Search the Word Study Manual

Volume I

B. Stuart, MEd PhD LCPC

Search the Word Study Manual

Volume I

This text is dedicated
to the
Pastor and members
of
Hope Redemption Worship Center, Inc.
Georgia.

"Study to show thyself approved unto God, a workman that needs not to

be ashamed, rightly dividing the word of truth"

II Timothy 2:15.

Search the Word Study Manual

Volume I

Copyright © 2013 B. Stuart, MEd PhD LCPC

Faith Restoration Ministries [FRM] International

www.frministry.org

Printed in the United States of America

ISBN-13:978-1491264638

Table of Contents

Preface

The aim of *Search the Word Study Manual* is to motivate God's people to get interested in His word, by spending time searching the Scriptures in order to have a deeper relationship with Him. Sometimes people attend a church for years, but still do not know what they believe. In fact, many cannot give even a reasonable description of why Jesus came to earth other than He died on the Cross. Most only attend church because their parents belonged to that particular assembly, but they themselves do not know what they believe.

Some people believe that living a good life, will take them to heaven and only bad people go to hell. Others believe that death is the end of all things and there is no heaven or hell. The Scriptures show that it goes much deeper than mere understanding that God is real, and that one will go to either heaven or hell. The truth is that each person must have a personal relationship with the Lord Jesus Christ to talk about Him or even to love Him. It is through knowing Jesus that we will be able to know God.

The study of God's word is vital to the life of every believer since it is from His word we learn about Him. God's word is the expression of His character. It reveals His love towards mankind, and His concern for our welfare.

It is in the word of God that we learn about heaven and hell so that we can aim for the one, and shun the other. When we study God's word, we understand that He forgives and forgets our sins. We learn that He is faithful and just to forgive us when we fail.

We further learn that He is kind, merciful and patient.

Although *Search the Word Study Manual* will not be able to capture all of God's character and work, yet it gives a semblance of who He is, and His constant care toward His children.

Jesus said, **Search the scriptures; for in them ye think ye have eternal life: and they are they which testify of me [John 5:39]**. It is from the word we will know about God. Therefore, if we do not read, understand, meditate, and apply His word, we will fall for all kinds of doctrines, which eventually will separate us from the truth. The word emphatically states, **Study to show thyself approved unto God, a workman that needs not to be ashamed, rightly dividing the word of truth [II Timothy 2:15]**.

From the desk of Pastor Winston L. Blair

All Scripture is given by inspiration of God, and is profitable for doctrine, for reproof, for correction, for instruction in righteousness: That the man of God may be perfect, thoroughly furnished unto all good works." II Timothy 3:16-17

Studying the Bible is an integral part of a Christian's relationship with God. As the Pastor of **Hope Redemption Worship Center**, one of my primary responsibilities is to teach the Bible.

Teaching the Scripture is a constant process imparting honest biblical teachings to the people of God, to provide them with the right information to know God and be prepared to work for God's ministry.

Our Sunday School Manual is designed to provide Biblical education and Christian principles, which are the foundation for building our Christianity.

I thank God for Dr. Stuart and her vision for this book. May God continue to bless her and inspire her to do His work.

Thank you Dr. Stuart, you are a blessing.

Pastor Winston L. Blair

About the Author

Dr. Stuart is a Licensed Clinical Pastoral Counselor [LCPC], ordained minister, and published author with many books for inspirational and educational development. The categories include counseling, leadership, and youth development. She is a professional conference speaker with program development, leadership, and organizational skills. She has a passion for the preservation of the Christian Marriage, and presents a weekly Internet program on issues and topics pertaining to the institution.

Her latest publication **Search the Word Study Manual, Volume 1** is a collection of messages and themes given through the Holy Spirit, which she has chosen to share with her readers.

The aim for preparing this manual is for the Adult Sunday Bible Study, which she teaches at **Hope Redemption Worship Center Inc.,** Georgia, where **Rev. Winston L. Blair** is pastor. It is her desire that the Lord will bless His people through these words, and that the gospel will continue to reach across the world.

Dr. Barbara
2013

Structure of the Manual

This first manual is set up in eight sections, each with different topics for discussion. This book is specifically for Bible Study discussions, small or large groups such as Sunday School, and Retreats.

Section 1, Foundational Ministries of the Church

Section 2, Spiritual Gifts for the Church

Section 3, Spiritual Growth

Section 4, Renounce Worldliness

Section 5, Your Vocation/Calling

Section 6, God's Protective Power

Section 7, False Teachers

Section 8, The Deceitfulness of Sin

Sections

Each Section has a number of lessons, which the teacher can use accordingly. There are no dates attached to the lessons, and the purpose for this is that teachers can switch according to the season.

Teaching Methods

Every teacher knows that no two classes are the same, and people differ in their personalities, desires, and opinions. Therefore, the teacher must choose a method of delivery, suitable for the class.

Teacher

Remember that the students are depending on you to answer their questions. Do research beforehand. Use Dictionaries, and Commentaries or whatever tool suitable for the lesson you will present.

If you do not know or have an answer, say so. Next, find out for the next time you meet so that you can help that student with the question.

Let the students do research and help themselves by preparing before coming to the class. In your delivery, get the students interested by bringing the lesson to life to motivate enthusiasm, attention, and stir up their minds. Ideas and opinions may differ, but you must know how to hold the class together and do not impose your ideas and beliefs. Always pray and commit all into the hands of the Holy Spirit.

Review

The review discussion questions are only suggestions, which the teacher may choose to use if he or she so desires. Always keep in mind that you, through the Holy Spirit, are in charge of your class or group.

Readiness

One of the traits of a successful teacher is readiness, and preparedness. Come ready to teach. Prepare your lesson beforehand with prayer and direction from the Holy Spirit. Keep in mind that you cannot do it by yourself, nor will the Holy Spirit do it all for you. He will **help**, but will not do all the work [Romans 8:26].

Section 1

Foundational Ministries for the Church

Although there are many who call themselves apostles and prophets in these modern times; nevertheless, many are only imposters looking for a title. These are people who are seeking prestige, and to elevate themselves in the Christian community. They are mere title-holders with no substance to prove their worth. In **Revelation 2:2**, we read, **I know thy works, and thy labour, and thy patience, and how thou canst not bear them which are evil: and thou hast tried them which say they are apostles, and are not, and hast found them liars**. Thou hast tried them which say they are apostles and are not, and hast found them liars should be taken very seriously by every leader; when someone presents credentials for a position in any of these ministries. This section discusses the five foundational ministries given to the church for its work and mission on earth.

   a. Apostle
   b. Prophets
   c. Evangelists
   d. Pastors
   e. Teachers

Foundational Ministries for the Church

Matthew 9:1-6, Mark 3:13-19, Luke 6:12-16, Acts 6:1-6, Ephesians 4:1-12

Introduction

Speaking of Jesus, the Scriptures reported that, **When he ascended up on high, he led captivity captive, and gave gifts unto men. And he gave some apostles; and some, prophets; and some, evangelists; and some, pastors and teachers** [**Ephesians 4:8, 11**]. These "gifts" refer to ministries in the local church to extend the gospel to all people across the nations. One could also use the term "instruments" because each ministry operates under the influence and power of the Holy Spirit. No one can minister effectively without the Holy Spirit's empowerment and guidance. The gifts were for the equipping of the saints to enable leaders to understand and interpret the doctrine of Christ in a cogent manner to *convince* sinners of their need for the Saviour, and lead them to repentance.

The gifts were not for any private acquisition nor should anyone display them for spiritual expertise.

Therefore, no leader should appoint anyone in any of the ministries without thorough search of the individual's readiness, maturity, and with evidence of his or her Christian walk with Christ.

Selecting Leaders

There are two specific passages indicating the process and qualities, before appointing someone in a ministerial office to serve God's people.

In the *first* instance, the disciples appointed **Matthias** to fill the empty position of Judas Iscariot [**Acts 1:15-26**]. This passage shows the process of selection by preceding with prayer, and enlisting the Holy Spirit's guidance and wisdom even though He was not mentioned. They prayed, **Thou, Lord, who knows the hearts of all men, show whether of these two thou hast chosen, that he may take part of this ministry and the apostleship**…. [**Acts 1:24-25**].

The *second* time occurred at the appointment of **deacons** [**Acts 6:1-6**]. They described the *qualities* in **Acts 6:3** stating, **Wherefore, brethren, look ye out among you seven men of honest report, full of the Holy Ghost and wisdom, whom we may appoint over this business.** The operative qualities are "**honest report**," "**full of the Holy Ghost**," and "**wisdom**." This is clear speech, which needs hardly any interpretation.

Evident also is the need for guidance, which they sought in prayer before making the selection. Clearly then, no leader should base spiritual appointment on friendship or nepotism as we see in the local churches of today.

Foundational Ministries for the Church

Church leaders must be careful of people who go around, as apostles, prophets, and bishops because some do not pastor a church or never had one, and may not even belong to a local church. Be wise when you are seeking someone to fill a position in the local church, specifically taking note of those who present impressive credentials. Do not appoint until you know the Holy Spirit has anointed that individual to such a position. It is better to wait and hear from God.

There can be no doubt then that each gift must come from God and operating through the Holy Spirit. No one should place himself or herself in an office because of a one-time enablement from the Holy Spirit. Each person must prove himself before holding an office.

All the Scriptures report that all spiritual gifts come through the Holy Spirit to help us in our work, and for us to remain stable with the Lord [**I Corinthians 12**]. Therefore, it is the duty of every Christian to secure and maintain a strong relationship with Him. This comes through our faith in God and making ourselves available to Him.

Since the gifts are for the benefit, administration, governing and mission of the church, there should be no hindrance for the active working of the gifts of the Spirit. It is important that every church encourage the operation of the gifts of the Spirit in its midst. However, for this section, the discussion will be about apostles, prophets, evangelists, pastors and teachers.

_____
_____
_____
_____
_____
_____
_____
_____
_____
_____
_____
_____
_____
_____
_____
_____
_____
_____

Lesson 1: Apostles

Matthew 28:18-28, Acts 2:38, Ephesians 4:11-12

The Great Commission

All power is given unto me in heaven and in earth. Go ye therefore, and teach all nations, baptizing them in the name of the Father, and of the Son, and of the Holy Ghost. Teaching them to observe all things whatsoever I have commanded you: and, lo, I am with you always, even unto the end of the world, [Matthew 28:18-28.

Repent, and be baptized every one of you in the Name of Jesus Christ for the remission of sins, and ye shall receive the gift of the Holy Ghost, [Acts 2:38].

The apostle is a special messenger or ambassador sent by God with a message to others in the faith, maybe a church or to plant churches in areas for the preaching of the gospel, and to make disciples of others [**Matthew 28:19**]. They are witnesses in the world who proclaim the gospel of Jesus Christ, to win souls for the Kingdom of God [**Acts 1:8**]. The apostle is commissioned with a particular task or role.

The Twelve Apostles were the foundation of the church. They planted churches, healed, and suffered for their faith in the Lord Jesus Christ. They interacted with the Lord Jesus face-to-face. From the teachings of those early apostles, we can continue with the mission of the church with the work they laid down for us to follow according to **Acts 2:42**, which states: **And they continued steadfastly in the apostles' doctrine and fellowship, and in breaking of bread, and in prayers**.

Moreover, an apostle is one who has had a personal contact with the Lord Jesus Christ; he functions in the ministry with *signs*, *wonders*, and *miracles*. This does not necessarily mean that everyone who does these things is automatically an apostle.

Referring to the office of an Apostle, there is no place in the New Testament church, where any of the Apostles designated anyone to be an Apostle. That authority belongs to Jesus Christ alone. We note the offices of **Bishops, I Timothy 3:1-7, Titus 1:7-8**; Elders, **I Timothy 5:17, 19, Titus 1:5**; and **Deacons, Acts 6:1-6, I Timothy 3:8**]. In fact, Jesus Christ is the Chief Apostle [**Hebrews 3:1**] and He designated this office with authority to **the Twelve** who were His witnesses. However, Paul was the **last** of the Apostles, who met with the Lord Jesus Christ on the Damascus Road, **[Acts 9, Corinthians 15:7-9, I Timothy 2:7]**. Persons who are going about today with the title "apostle" are imposters. There is no merit to the title they hold.

If you were not called, anointed, and appointed by Jesus Christ to be an apostle, leave it alone. Moreover, even though you may have planted churches and seen various things happen in your ministry, **it does not make you an Apostle**. Personally, I do not think anyone should be going around posing as an apostle or in any office for which he or she was not anointed and appointed to hold. What is most important is that we continue evangelizing and obeying the word of God through those teachings laid down by the true apostles.

All apostles are evangelists, but not all evangelists are apostles.

Lesson 2: Prophets

Numbers 12:6-8, Deuteronomy 13:1-5, Jeremiah 14:13-16, 23:9-40, I Corinthians 14:29-32

Introduction

And God hath set some in the church, first apostles, secondarily prophets, thirdly teachers, after that miracles, then gifts of healings, helps, governments, diversities of tongues [I Corinthians 12:28].

Follow after charity, and desire spiritual gifts, but rather that ye may prophesy [I Corinthians 14:1].

God sets the office of the prophet in the church along with the apostles, teachers and others [**I Corinthians 12:28**. In **Ephesians 4:11**], the office of the prophet is one of the foundational gifts to the church, but the Holy Spirit empowers the individual as he or she utters a message [**I Corinthians 12:4-6**]. Clearly: Father, Son, and Holy Spirit are in harmony concerning the *office*, *function*, and *administration* of the prophet.

There are people who do not believe the office of the prophet is necessary, especially when compared to the true prophets of old such as *Elijah*, *Elisha*, *Jeremiah*, and so on. They prophesied what God gave them. The majority of those who call themselves prophets today seem to be agents of materialism, whom I call fortune-tellers.

This does not say there are no true prophets of today. There are, but they are few. They are the ones who operate in obscurity unlike the deceivers who are plentiful, materially rich and financially successful, found all around. They are always spitting out prosperity to impress, but for the most part one could ask how many of those messages do come to fruition. Therefore, anyone who claims to be a prophet must give proof to that calling with evidence. Additionally, the Holy Spirit selects those whom He desires to fit in any office.

Description of a Prophet

The prophet declares truths through the Holy Spirit, by forth-telling the <u>will</u> and <u>counsel</u> of God [**Luke 1:67-79**]. The prophet is someone through whom God speaks [**Numbers 12:2**]. He receives messages for God's people for <u>edification</u>, <u>exhortation</u>, and <u>comfort</u> [**I Corinthians 14:3**]. Nevertheless, for the prophet to be effective, he must walk consistently in the gift similar to a doctor or all other professionals.

Another note is that the gift of prophesying is from the Holy Spirit, and any believer can prophesy if the Holy Spirit gives the permission.

However, when the prophet delivers a message, it "**serves not for them that believe not, but for them which believe**" [**I Corinthians 14:22b**].

Here are some very important points to note

[a]. While someone may prophesy, this does not place the person in the office of a prophet. It could be a natural gift, which the individual received at birth;

[b]. Another view, is that someone may use logic or commonsense to predict something that happens, but it does not make him or her, a prophet;

[c]. The true prophet receives this gift from God through the Holy Spirit, and functions in that position. It is his or her work, position, office. Examples are Elijah, Elisha, Isaiah, Jeremiah, and many others.

Too many [want-to-be-prophets] have missed these most important points, and have made the mistake by calling themselves prophets. The Holy Spirit can and will empower anyone, at any time to give a prophetic word, but this impartation does not make the person a prophet.

Identifying False Prophets

According to [**Deuteronomy 13:1-3**]

If there arise among you a prophet, or a dreamer of dreams, and gives thee a sign or a wonder, [1] **And the sign or the wonder come to pass, whereof he spoke unto thee, saying, Let us go after other gods, which thou has not known, and let us serve them;** [2] **Thou shalt not hearken unto the words of that prophet, or that dreamer of dreams: for the Lord your God proves you, to know whether ye love the Lord your God with all your heart and with all your soul.** [3]

This is clear speech followed by a warning in [**Deuteronomy 13:5**] and the consequences to follow the message of the false prophets.

In **Jeremiah 14:13-14**, God defends Himself stating:

Then said I, Ah, Lord God! Behold, the prophets say unto them, Ye shall not see the sword, neither shall ye have famine; but I will give you assured peace in this place. [13]

God's response: **The prophets prophesy lies in my name: I sent them not, neither have I commanded them, neither spoke unto them: they prophesy unto you a false vision and divination, and a thing of naught, and the deceit of their heart." [14]**

Divination: *qesem*, This is a false vision, a thing of naught, and the deceit of the heart. Similar to fortune telling

The passage continues with warning from **verse 15-18**; similar to God's warning in **Deuteronomy 13**. The word of God warns, **It is a fearful thing to fall into the hands of the living God, [Hebrews 10:31]**. Liars and deceivers will be exposed for their deception and lying upon God.

So-called prophets of today only prophesy prosperity. I have yet to meet someone who shows up the sins of God's people, or even warn them of preparing for the coming of the Lord Jesus Christ. Sadly, many want-to-get-rich-quick people are buying into their deceit. Surely, they will all fall headlong into the fiery furnace where all liars will be **[Revelation 21:8]**.

False prophets pervert the word of God. They are phonies who are hypocrites and operate under a mask. Jesus warned about them in **Matthew 24**. There will be more on false teachers in another section. Hear what God said in **Jeremiah 23:14, 16, I have seen also in the prophets of Jerusalem an horrible thing: they commit adultery, and walk in lies: they strengthen also the hands of evildoers, that none doth return from his wickedness: they are all of them unto me as Sodom, and the inhabitants thereof as Gomorrah. [14]**

Thus saith the Lord of hosts, Hearken not unto the words of the prophets that prophesy unto you: they make you vain: they speak a vision of their own heart, and not out of the mouth of the Lord [16]. God will expose false prophets in His own time and will reprimand them for dishonouring His name.

The True Prophet of God

According to the word of God concerning the true prophet: **Hear now my words: If there be a prophet among you, I the Lord will make myself known unto him in a vision, and will speak unto him in a dream [Numbers 12:6]**.

Furthermore, the word states, **I will raise them up a Prophet from among their brethren, like unto thee, and will put my words in his mouth; and he shall speak unto them all that I shall command him [Deuteronomy 18:18]**.

A true prophet called by God will have signs following his message. **When a prophet speaks in the name of the Lord, if the thing follow not, nor come to pass, that is the thing which the Lord hath not spoken, but the prophet hath spoken it presumptuously: thou shalt not be afraid of him, [Deuteronomy 18:22]**. God's word will not fall to the ground. The word spoken by the true prophet of God will accomplish and fulfill its mission.

The true prophet proclaims or gives a message he receives from the Lord. He announces and heralds God's word **I Samuel 3:20**. God will always stand by His word, and will not support those who prophesy lies or out of their emotions **[Jeremiah 23:14, 16, 21-40]**.

The life of the prophet of God is characterized by holiness. Therefore, he must be in close communion with God. God reveals His purpose and messages to that person for the church. The message of the prophet is not mainly for prediction, but rather to declare the will of God whether for an individual or for the church.

Uniqueness of the True Prophet

The prophet of God must be in active communication with Him to receive insight into divine secrets or mysteries, and to communicate those messages to others. The prophet does not guess when it comes to the will of God. He does not pre-suppose [**assumes** or **presumes: guesses, imagines, or takes liberty into God's domain**] concerning what might happen. Instead, he listens and conveys messages to the hearers. In Old Testament times, those prophets prophesied about the salvation that was to come, and those who strayed away from God calling them to repentance. However, since Jesus came, prophesy is publishing of the word through preaching, and teaching.

Office of the Prophet

The office of the prophet is a gift similar to all others given by the Holy Spirit, which relates to all believers who possess this gift [**I Thessalonians 5:20**].

Function of the Prophet

The function of the prophet is to encourage the church for *edification*, *exhortation*, and *comfort* for all [**I Corinthians 14:3-4**]. Here is an important word: Although someone prophesies, he does not necessarily holds, the office of a prophet. Prophets are placed alongside the Apostles in the foundation of the New Testament Church [**Ephesians 2:20, 3:5**].

Discussion

i. Are prophets the same as fortune-tellers? What are the differences if there are?

ii. How can you tell if someone heard from God?

iii. What do you need to do test the true prophet from the phony?

iv. Why do you think there are so many who call themselves prophets today?

v. Should the church encourage prophesying?

vi. How does God respond to false prophets?

vii. Should anyone fear God's warnings about using His name falsely?

viii. What should the prophet do when he receives a word from God while in a church service?

Use Scriptures to support your responses.

Suggestions for further reading

i. Numbers 12

ii. Deuteronomy18

iii. Isaiah 55

iv. Jeremiah 14, 23

v. Jeremiah 18:22

vi. I Corinthians 14:29-32

Lesson 3: Evangelists

Matthew 10:1-15, Mark 3:13-19, Luke 9:1-6, Acts 1:7-8, II Timothy 4:1-8

Function and Office of the Evangelist

II Timothy 4:1-5

I charge thee therefore before God, and the Lord Jesus Christ, who shall judge the quick and the dead at his appearing and his kingdom; [1]

Preach the word; be instant in season, out of season; reprove, rebuke, exhort with all long-suffering and doctrine. [2]

For the time will come when they will not endure sound doctrine; but after their own lusts shall they heap to themselves teachers, having itching ears; [3]

And they shall turn away their ears from the truth, and shall be turned unto fables. [4]

But watch thou in all things, endure afflictions, do the work of an evangelist, make full proof of thy ministry. [5]

Paul, in the passage above was clear in his teachings concerning the work of the evangelist. He showed that it required discipline for difficult believers; teaching believers about personal responsibilities; honesty concerning the faith; stability to the calling, faithfulness to the calling, knowledge of the true word of God, and being an example with evidence. He also referred to the element of suffering, which the evangelist may face. Probably, Paul alluded to his own experience and persecutions, which he suffered. Nevertheless, he encouraged the evangelist **to endure afflictions, do the work of an evangelist [5]**.

The evangelist is one who proclaims the good news of salvation to the world. If you are called and ordained to be an evangelist, you must **be ready always to give an answer concerning the hope that is in you with meekness and fear** [I Peter 3:15]. It means you must not fail to attest to what you believe with humility and reverential fear.

The work of the evangelist is evangelism, which means reaching people everywhere. Jesus commissioned, **Go ye therefore, and teach all nations, baptizing them in the name of the Father, and of the Son, and of the Holy Ghost: Teaching them to observe all things whatsoever I have commanded you: and, lo, I am with you always, even unto the end of the world** [Matthew 28:19-20].

The evangelist will not develop his ministry all at once. Instead, the ministry is a process, which affects the very lifestyle of the individual. No one should consider one experience of success as a calling to be an evangelist, or for any office. **Ministry is not a desire, but a calling or vocation**.

Although apostles are messengers to the world, so are evangelists. Evangelists could be considered missionaries, who proclaim the gospel anywhere and at any time. Nevertheless, the title of evangelist denotes a *function* and not an office [*it is not a title – instead, it is work or function* [**Phillip** - **Acts 8:5**]. Evangelists were subordinate to the apostles and prophets.

> *All apostles can be evangelists, but not all evangelists may be apostles*.

Discussion

   i.   Describe the work of any evangelist you have known.

   ii.   What signs or evidences do you believe would identify an evangelist?

   iii.   Does the evangelist have to leave his hometown to do evangelism?

   iv.   Can you identify any evangelists in the New Testament Church?

   v.   Since we have the television, radio, and internet, do you think the work of the evangelist is necessary anymore?

_____

_____

_____

_____

_____

_____

_____

_____

_____

_____

_____

_____

_____

_____

Lesson 4: Pastors

Jeremiah 3:15, Acts 20:28-32, II Timothy 2:24-26

Introduction

II Timothy 2:24-26

The servant of the Lord must not strive; but be gentle unto all men, apt to teach, patient, [24]

In meekness instructing those that oppose themselves; if God peradventure will give them repentance to the acknowledging of the truth; [25]

And that they may recover themselves out of the snare of the devil, who are taken captive by him at his will. [26]

And I will give you pastors according to mine own heart, which shall feed you with knowledge and understanding [Jeremiah 3:15].

Take heed therefore unto yourselves, and to all the flock, over the which the Holy Ghost hath made you overseers, to feed the church of God, which he hath purchased with his own blood [Acts 20:28].

The office of the pastor is a high calling, which requires dedication and faithfulness. No one should take on this position without being called. First, the pastor must bear in mind that sometimes the experience can be thankless and demanding. Despite the difficulties of his job, he must depend upon the Holy Spirit to take him through each situation. Second, people are different, and no two members are the same because each person has different personalities and needs. Finally, members come from different backgrounds, culture and so many other factors, which makes the calling sometimes challenging.

Functions of the Pastor

The admonitions above, appeal to pastors, that they guard the people of God and protect them from wolves, such as false teachers. Evidently, the pastor is the under-shepherd [Jesus is the Chief Shepherd, I Peter 5:4] of the sheep.

1. He should, **Feed the flock of God which is among you, taking the oversight thereof, not by constraint, but willingly; not for filthy lucre, but of a ready mind [I Peter 5:2].** God will call, ordain, and appoint His pastors [**Jeremiah 3:15**].

2. Similar to all other ministries and calling, each person should make sure he or she fits the office of a pastor. There are many deceivers, who **assume** the role of pastor, but were never called and appointed by God.

3. Including in the pastor's role is visiting the sick and checking on members who are missing.

4. He should guard, guide, teach, train and nurture the flock [the people of God].

5. He should not treat God's people with coercion or disdain.

6. It is the duty of the pastor to discipline, and instruct so that members follow guidelines, to help them mature in the ministry.

7. The pastor must be a visionary and leader, who will select and train others to work alongside him in carrying out the mission of the church/gospel.

8. He should perform spiritual ceremonies such as weddings, communion, baptisms, the dedication of babies, and funerals.

9. He should be available to encourage family members after the loss of a loved one, and other crises situations; such as after divorce and other life-changing situations.

10. Apart from preaching, the pastor's duty is to counsel. It is very important for a pastor to have some knowledge of counseling to help those who are in crisis, and who need immediate help.

Discussion
  i. What is the purpose and function of a pastor?
  ii. Can anyone be a pastor without being called by God?
  iii. Do you think a pastor can also be a prophet, apostle, or evangelist?
  iv. Describe some of the qualities of a pastor.

_____
_____
_____
_____
_____
_____
_____

Lesson 5: Teachers

II Chronicles 1:6-12, Ezekiel 44:23

_____

Introduction

This book of the law shall not depart out of thy mouth; but thou shalt meditate therein day and night, that thou mayest observe to do according to all that is written therein: for then thou shalt make thy way prosperous, and then thou shalt have good success [Joshua 1:8].

Teachers have a distinct function to interpret the word of God, so that believers understand the doctrine to avoid being led astray with heresies [**Acts 13:1**]. Nevertheless, similar to Solomon, they should seek wisdom from God if they are to be successful.

To teach: to instruct, direct, guide, and to relate truth.

In many churches, teachers work in the department of Christian Education. They prepare, coordinate, and teach mainly in the Sunday School. The teacher is a great asset to the pastor because he will relieve him from teaching on a Sunday morning, and later may have to deliver the message for the day.

Many pastors are over-worked because there is a lack of spiritually qualified workers. Sometimes there is difficulty to assign someone to the role of Sunday School teacher. Nevertheless, it is always important to ensure the individual is <u>spiritually</u> qualified, willing, and available.

Although there may be a need for a teacher, the pastor should not position anyone without seeking the direction and guidance of the Holy Spirit, even if that person is highly educated. What is most important is that the individual loves God's people and has the spiritual attributes, experiences, and abilities to fit into the position of teaching.

The office of Teachers

Teachers are spiritual leaders who have the responsibility to teach the people of God and lead them into the right path. They should <u>instruct</u> and <u>train</u> the people to assume responsibilities as they work in the ministry. Some spiritual teachers teach in Bible Colleges, and other para-church organizations.

In [**I Corinthians 12:28**], teachers are held in the same category as apostles and prophets. The teacher has the duty of giving instruction relating to the word of God to the people. Therefore, teachers can be pastors and pastors can perform the role of teaching. Both pastors and teachers could be one person.

However, there are spiritual persons who are apologetics. They research, study, and interpret truth and certainty of the Bible with evidence to support their findings. From those persons we have spiritual commentaries and biblical dictionaries.

Be an Example

Let us not forget that teaching does not necessarily have to be by word of mouth, but by the way we live, and the demonstration of our character before the world. Jesus said, **Let your light so shine before men, that they may see your good works, and glorify your Father which is in heaven** [Matthew 5:16].

The title of teacher was used as a mark of respect when antagonists tried to entrap Jesus in **Matthew 22:15-16** [*master here means teacher*]. This form of address was also given to Jewish scribes in **Luke 2:46**, [*doctors in this verse meant teachers*].

Suggestions for further reading

a. Exodus 31:1-11
b. Joshua 1
c. I Chronicles 28:9-10
d. II Chronicles 1:1-10
e. Jeremiah 3:15
f. Jeremiah 14:13-18
g. Luke 9:23-26, 57-62
h. Acts 2:43
i. Acts 5:12
j. I Corinthians 12
k. II Corinthians 12:12
l. Ephesians 4:11
m. I Timothy 2:7

Discussion

1. Describe the qualities identified required in an individual who desires to minister?
2. There are many people going around as prophets, but they are only prophesying prosperity, do you trust them?
3. Can a teacher fill the position of pastor?
4. Explain the functions of apostles, prophets, evangelists, pastors, and teachers.
5. What does it means by being "lords over God's heritage."
6. Do all pastors have to go to a Bible School? Why should a pastor attend a Bible School?

_____

_____

_____

_____

_____

_____

_____

Foundational Ministries for the Church

Section 2

Spiritual Gifts for the Church

The Holy Spirit inspires all spiritual gifts. He is the one who gives the power for the individual to perform in the gift he or she has. Spiritual gifts are specifically given to the church to accomplish the work of the ministry, and to nurture the believers.

Ephesians 1:12-14, That we should be to the praise of his glory, who first trusted in Christ. [12] In whom ye also (trusted), after that ye heard the word of truth, the gospel of your salvation: in whom also after that ye believed, ye were sealed with that Holy Spirit of promise, [13] Which is the earnest of our inheritance until the redemption of the purchased possession, unto the praise of his glory]. [14]

Whatever the gift might be, the individual must perform his duty with the inspiration and guidance of the Holy Spirit. It is the indwelling Holy Spirit who will help the believer live above sin. [**Galatians 5:16; This I say then, walk in the Spirit, and ye shall not fulfill the lust of the flesh**].

This section discusses the Spiritual Gifts for the Church:

a. Introduction

b. Diversities of Gifts

c. The Holy Spirit

d. Purpose for the Gifts

e. The Importance of the Gifts

f. The Influence of the Gifts

Spiritual Gifts for the Church

Romans 12:6-8, I Corinthians 12, Ephesians 4:11-12

Introduction

Gifts given by Jesus Christ

[Ephesians 4:8, Wherefore he saith, When he ascended up on high, he led captivity captive, and gave gifts unto men].

Gift: *charisma*, a gift of grace, free, divine gratuity, spiritual endowment, miraculous faculty.

There are five specific offices or ministries for the <u>foundation</u> and <u>structure</u> of the church, stated in **Ephesians 4:11-12**

And he gave some apostles; and some, prophets; and some evangelists; and some, pastors and teachers; [11] [*Discussed above in the first section*].

For the perfecting of the saints, for the work of the ministry, for the edifying of the body of Christ. [12].

[I Corinthians 12:28], And God has set some in the church, first apostles, secondarily prophets, thirdly teachers, after that miracles, then gifts of healings, helps, governments, diversities of tongues."

Notice that all are in the plural, which means no one person has any gift to himself or herself. It is very important that leaders are careful when selecting individuals for these positions. It should not be a random effort for the benefit of titling someone.

Gifts given by God

[Romans 12:6-8, Having then gifts differing according to the grace that is given to us, whether prophecy, let us prophesy according to the proportion of faith; [6]

Or ministry, let us wait on our ministering: of he that teaches, on teaching; [7]

Or he that exhorts, on exhortation: he that gives let him do it with diligence; he that shows mercy, with cheerfulness. [8]

The foregoing shows that each gift needs time to mature. Therefore, the evidence of the gift is a process, which the individual must prepare and each day allow the Holy Spirit to direct and guide as development in that calling takes place. No one should be in a hurry. Rather, patience, guidance, wisdom and the anointing are vital for success.

Gifts from the Holy Spirit I Corinthians 12:8-11

For to one is given by the Spirit the word of wisdom; to another the word of knowledge by the same Spirit; [8]

To another faith by the same Spirit; to another the gifts of healing by the same Spirit; [9]

To another the working of miracles; to another prophecy; to another discerning of spirits; to another divers kinds of tongues; to another the interpretation of tongues; [10

But all these work that one and selfsame Spirit, dividing to every man severally as he will. [11]

_____
_____
_____
_____
_____
_____
_____
_____
_____
_____
_____
_____
_____
_____
_____
_____
_____
_____
_____
_____
_____
_____
_____
_____
_____
_____
_____

Lesson 1: Diversities of Gifts

I Corinthians 12:4-11, I John 1:5-10

Introduction t

I Corinthians 12:4-7ff

Now there are diversities of gifts, but the same Spirit. [4]

And there are differences of administrations, but the same Lord. [5]

And there are diversities of operations, but it is the same God which works (*all in all*). [6]

But the manifestation of the Spirit is given to every man to profit withal. [7]. *Withal,* means *to profit all*.

In the passage above, Paul acknowledged the godhead: Father, Son, and Holy Ghost. In fact, Paul was very diligent in doing this in his epistles. Jesus Himself, always include the Father and showed high regard for Him. It could be that since the diversities of gifts came through each administration of the godhead, he was willing to keep this intact.

Diversities of gifts means there are many different gifts. No two gifts are the same, but they each operate under the inspiration and empowerment of the Holy Spirit [**Now there are diversities of gifts, but the same Spirit, I Corinthians 12:4**].

There are different types, administrations, and operations, but each works through the Holy Spirit. Similar to the members of the body, which work in unison, the gifts given to the church must all work in agreement with each other.

If each person is obedient to the Holy Spirit, there will be no conflict or incongruence with the working of the gifts for the edification, and development of the members. Instead, there will be unity, rather than discord.

I John 1:5-7ff

This then is the message which we have heard of him, and declare unto you, that God is light, and in him is no darkness at all. [5]

If we say we have fellowship with him, and walk in darkness, we lie, and do not the truth: [6]

The Gifts must work in Harmony

But if we walk in the light, as he is in the light, we have fellowship one with another, and the blood of Jesus Christ His Son cleanses us from all sin. [7]

Another most important point is that the gifts are not for any personal interpretation or function, but each gift serves whereby all the members can profit, and this will enable growth in the church. In every corporation, or organization, there are all kinds of professional and non-professional people, who work together for the success of the entity. When there are problems, these sometimes cause delay.

There is no difference in the church. God expects each individual to work in unison to accomplish the mission of preaching the gospel and bringing souls into the kingdom.

Another factor is that similar to our bodies with its different members; each gift must work in accordance with the other, and so must the church of Jesus Christ with the different gifts. We must work together, and not independent of one another. Moreover, without those gifts in the church, it cannot operate. Is it any wonder, that God in His wisdom gave so many gifts to the church?

Reliance on each Other

Each gift has its own purpose and must not inhibit another. Therefore, each individual must be careful to adhere to the principles of abiding in obedience to the word of God for unity. Discord does not come from out of the air. Consequently, if we all obey the teaching of **Endeavouring to keep the unity of the Spirit in the bond of peace [Ephesians 4:3];** surely indeed, peace will exist among us.

The Bible teaches, **Depart from evil, and do good; seek peace, and pursue it [Psalm 37:14].** This tells us that every believer must seek to work together for the benefit of each other, even though we will often face various types of oppositions and differences. Nevertheless, this should not hinder growth and development if the gifts of the Holy Spirit are actively in operation.

Clearly then, we can understand why there are diversities of gifts for the administration and operation of the church. God is wise and knows all that we need beforehand. For this reason, there should be no schism in the body if each person conducts himself or herself in a manner, which depicts Christianity and godliness.

Diversities of gifts are for the administration and operation of the church. Despite the diversities, they all operate under the inspiration and guidance of the Holy Spirit.

_____

_____

_____

_____

Spiritual Gifts for the Church

Suggestions for further reading

i. I Corinthians 1:10-17
ii. I Corinthians 12
iii. II Timothy 2:14-26
iv. I John 3:1-3
v. I John 1:5-10
vi. I Peter 2

Discussion

i. Why do you think there are so many gifts, but different administrations and operations?
ii. Why should each leader endeavour to have the gifts in operation in the local church?
iii. What might happen if individuals are prevented from using the gifts allotted to the local church?
iv. How can an individual identify his or her gift?

_____
_____
_____

Lesson 2: Purpose for the Gifts

Ephesians 4:12-13, I Thessalonians 4:1-12, I Corinthians 10-17

A. For the Perfecting of the Saints

Ephesians 4:12-13, For the perfecting of the saints, for the work of the ministry, for the edifying of the body of Christ:

Till we all come in the unity of the faith, and the knowledge of the Son of God, unto a perfect man, unto the measure of the stature of the fullness of Christ.

Perfecting of the saints means, making them fit and ready each day to face the challenges of the Christian life. It includes the activity of training, teaching, and preparing them for service in the ministry. It means preparing the saints for growth, spiritual warfare, ministry, and with what it takes to be a successful Christian. However, no believer becomes mature immediately at conversion. For this reason, every pastor should spend time to teach the members the doctrine of Christ, and major principles critical to the faith.

Despite the pastor's duty, each member **must** ensure that he or she seeks personal development in the faith. No one should coerce a member to secure strength and maturity. Everyone should have the desire for improvement and seeking a closer walk with the Lord each day. Jesus said, **If any man will come after me, let him deny himself, and take up his cross daily, and follow me, [Luke 9:23].** Evidently, growth requires <u>personal involvement</u>, <u>responsibility</u>, and <u>effort</u>.

To be perfect means to be complete, and denotes maturity. Since we are complete in Christ Jesus He has everything we need for development and maturity in Him [**Colossians 2:9-10, *read***]. Maturity means the constant work of sanctification through the Holy Spirit.

In order to be perfect, individually we must study the word of God to learn about Him, and to receive revelations and messages from Him.

[**II Timothy 2:15, Study to show thyself approved of God, a workman that need not to be ashamed, rightly dividing the word of truth**], <u>this verse cannot be over emphasized</u>.

Sanctification [I Thessalonians 4:3-12]

Sanctification is a quality and process vital for helping us grow towards perfection. It means we must be set apart by the Holy Spirit who will enable us to live holy as God intends us to do [**I Peter 1:15-16 read**].

In **II Thessalonians 2:13**, we read, **But we are bound to give thanks always to God for you, brethren beloved of the Lord, because God hath from the beginning chosen you to salvation through sanctification of the Spirit and belief of the truth**.

> **Sanctification:** *hágion*, holiness. To be set apart for God. It cannot be done unless the individual separates himself from fellowship with the world, and seek fellowship with God.

There can be no dispute that the evidence of the sanctified life will be seen as we interact with others, and by the way we handle problems. Sanctification takes place through the Holy Spirit, and we are sanctified in Christ [**I Corinthians 1:2**].

The work of sanctification is a process and continues throughout the life of the believer, involving the behaviour, and reflecting in the character. Therefore, it will influence our *body*, *soul*, and *spirit*.

The individual who endeavours to live a sanctified life will abstain from worldly attractions including illicit sexual sins and uncleanness relating to this activity [**Galatians 5:19-21, Colossians 3:5-9, read**]. That person depends on the Holy Spirit each day for guidance and direction [**Galatians 6:16, 24**]. The distinguishing evidence will also be seen in the fruits the individual produce [**Galatians 5:22-23**].

Consequently, the fundamental distinguishing features of sanctification are a life of holiness, separation, consecration, devotion to God, and abstaining from worldliness and its attractions.

B. For The Work of the Ministry

When we think of the ministry, it is safe to say that all born again believers are ministers. The reason is that we all, through the empowerment of Holy Spirit, administer the gifts for the benefit of edification, growth, development, and strengthening of the Body of Christ. Not everyone may be officially ordained a minister, but the Holy Spirit empowers each believer to do anything He chooses at any time.

Romans 12:4-5ff

For as we have many members in one body, and all members have not the same office: [4]
So we, (*being*) many, are one body in Christ, and every one members one of another. [5]
This passage clarifies the understanding that we are all ministers, and that we need each other for encouragement and support.

The title of minister does not only refer to those who are spiritual professionals and ordained, but everyone who is in Christ, and who is living in obedience to the word.

The work of the ministry means following the commission of Jesus Christ in **Matthew 28:19-20**, in order to spread the gospel. Similar to being qualified for secular work, in the church community, we must have spiritual qualifications to operate effectively in the ministry.

Ministry is not only preaching and teaching, but also refers to showing compassion to others and especially those who are weakest among us [**James 2**]. The demonstration of every gift must be with humility and Christ-likeness. Obviously, ministry means work, labour, love, showing mercy, kindness and so many other qualities such as are mentioned in **Galatians 5:22-23 – the fruit of the Spirit.**

Consequently, no gift is for any personal gratification, or boasting to cause others who do not have the same, to feel uncomfortable. Whatever our gift might be, let us keep in mind that this was given by the Holy Spirit. It was not because of our great spirituality or because of who we think we are, but because of God's great love toward us. **[Ephesians 2:4-5ff, But God, who is rich in mercy, for his great love wherewith he loved us, Even when we were dead in sins, hath quickened us together with Christ, (by grace ye are saved)]**.

Moreover, the gifts are selective, and the people who possess them are selective because there are different types of gifts, but all come from, and operates through the Holy Spirit's power and direction [**I Corinthians 12:4-6**]. This means that no one will possess all the gifts. Each person receives a gift or gifts, according to the discretion of the Holy Spirit, and His desire for the individual.

Therefore, since we are members of one Body; Jesus Christ being the Head, the gifts must be used for the purpose of the ministry. Whatever the Lord calls us to do our aim must be to improve ourselves individually and collectively, and to spread the gospel of Jesus Christ. Clearly then, the pastor must allow the gifts of the Holy Spirit to operate in the church as the Spirit gives utterance.

C. For Edification of the Body of Christ

To edify means to educate, instruct, and teach in order to build up and make people better. In the ministry, we can edify one another in many ways. We have the word of God, commentaries, dictionaries, prayer and intercession, teaching and direct revelation.

Nevertheless, this cannot take place without the empowerment of the Holy Spirit.

[Romans 8:26, Likewise the Spirit also helps our infirmities: for we know not what we should pray for as we ought: but the Spirit itself makes intercession for us with groanings which cannot be uttered].

The edification of the Body of Christ means to build up one another through internal strengthening. We need each other, and no one should operate on his or her own.

Prophecy is a gift for the edification of the church [**I Corinthians 14:22b**]. Therefore, if he or she is a true prophet, the message should build up the Body and strengthen the faith of the believers.

Division hurts the Body [I Corinthians1:10-17]

Now I beseech you, brethren, by the name of our Lord Jesus Christ, (*that*) ye all speak the same thing, and (*that*) there be no divisions among; but that ye be perfectly joined together in the same mind and in the same judgment. [10]

Unless we work together, the enemy will destroy us through wrong assessment and judgment of each other, which often result in separation, hostility, strife, and all manner of destructive behaviours.

Again, Paul admonished the believers about the importance of unity among us in [**Romans 16:17-18**], stating, **Now I beseech you brethren, mark them which cause divisions and offences contrary to the doctrine which ye have learned; and avoid them. [17]**

For they that are such serve not our Lord Jesus Christ, but their own belly; and by good words and fair speeches deceive the hearts of the simple. [18]

He further warned, **That there should be no schism [*division*] in the body; but that the members should have the same care one for another** [I Corinthians 12:25].

Division would only occur if there is <u>jealousy</u> in the midst or if there is <u>arrogance</u> against those who do not possess similar gifts as another member does.

How do we edify one another?

Paul wrote, **How is it then, brethren? When ye come together, every one of you has a psalm, has a doctrine, has a tongue, has a revelation, has an interpretation. Let all things be done unto edifying,** [**I Corinthians 14:26**].

The evidence is in the word that whatever we as believers do, should be for edification. [**II Corinthians 12:19b, but we do all things, dearly beloved, for your edifying**]. Therefore, it is the duty of every leader to identify spiritual gifts in the church, and encourage their operation to build up the Body of Jesus Christ. Nevertheless, believers must live in close relationship with the Lord, so that the Holy Spirit will find opportunities for imparting gifts to each life.

Discussion

i. In what ways does Romans 12:4-8, shows that each believer is a minister?

ii. How can the gifts of the Spirit edify the church or even a believer?

iii. What are some gifts, which are evident in the local church?

iv. If members do not co-operate, what is one of the main things that could happen to the church?

v. What are some of the ways Paul said we should edify one another?

vi. What is sanctification? How can we live sanctified lives?

vii. If someone is speaking in tongues and there is no interpreter, what should the pastor do?

Suggestions for further reading

i. Romans 12

ii. I Corinthians 12

iii. I Corinthians 14

iv. Ephesians

v. I Thessalonians 4:3-12

vi. James 2

Lesson 3: Factors Pertaining to the Gifts
[I Corinthians 12:12-18ff]

Referring to the gifts, Paul noted, **But all these work with that one and the selfsame Spirit, dividing to every man severally as he will [I Corinthians 12:11].** Paul further spoke of the significance of all gifts **in reference to the workings of the body [I Corinthians 12:12-31].** He wanted us to see how important each gift is to the other, and that we cannot work independently of each other since we are members of the same body.

The Importance of Each Member in the Body [I Corinthians 12:22-25]

Nay, much more those members of the body, which seem to be more feeble, are necessary: [22] And those (*members*) of the body, which we think to be less honourable, upon these we bestow more abundant honour; and our uncomely (*parts*) have more abundant comeliness. [23]

For our comely (*parts*) have no need: but God hath tempered the body together, having given more abundant honour to that (*part*) which lacked: [24]

> **Schism:** *schisma*, to split, tear, causing division, to sever, to make a rent.
> Think of *schizophrenia*, which is a splitting of mental functions.

That there should be no schism in the body; but that the members should have the same care one for another. [25]

Paul's aim was to <u>encourage unity</u>, <u>consistency of labour</u>, and the <u>need for each other</u> since no one gift is more important than the other. Although each gift is distinct and functions differently, yet they must work in unison with each other for the successful operation of the church. Similar to the body, which needs all its members to function in accordance for the benefit of the whole, in the church, each gift must work in agreement with one another.

Distinctiveness – but the same Spirit

Each gift is unique; but cannot work independently of the others because no one has **all** the gifts. Instead the Holy Spirit gives to each one as He sees fit for the benefit of each other in the Body of Christ **[I Corinthians 12:11, 18].** It is true that similar to the physical body, there are those who have certain gifts that might seem more important, but even those, which may not seem as important are vital for the effectual working of the ministry.

The Influence of the Gifts

Matthew 5:13-16

Ye are the salt of the earth: but if the salt have lost his savour, wherewith shall it be salted? It is thenceforth good for nothing, but to be cast out, and to be trodden under foot of men. [13]

Ye are the light of the world. A city that is set on an hill cannot be hid. [14]

Neither do men light a candle, and put it under a bushel, but on a candlestick: and it gives light unto all that are in the house. [15]

Let your light so shine before men, that they may see your good works, and glorify your Father which is in heaven. [16]

The effect of the gifts is revealed in the lives of the "True woman or man of God." The gifts should change the life of every believer to make him or her, a better person. It is the quality and substance of their lives that will demonstrate those gifts as the Holy Spirit gives utterance. This evidence is in character, trust, holiness, spiritual ethics, faithfulness, obedience, reliability, and humility.

1. **Proverbs 3:5-6 – *Trust in God***: That individual trusts God and does not depend on intellectual abilities or worldly philosophies.
2. **Isaiah 6:5-8, Psalm 51:10 - *Holiness***: Recognizes the need for God and cleansing of the heart. The aim is for holiness in order to please God.
3. **Isaiah 33:15, Psalm 15, 24 – *Spiritual Ethics***: Acknowledge righteousness, truthfulness, honesty, and being compassionate. The ethical person does not oppress, does not seek for gain or take bribes, does not cause harm, avoids evil, and seeks for justice for all. He or she is fair, humble, faithful, obedient, loyal, and reliable.
4. **Micah 6:8 – *Faithfulness***: The person called by God is merciful, does not hold a grudge. There is forgiveness, kindness, love, loyalty, and fairness.
5. **Galatians 5:16, 25 – *Obedience***: There is evidence of a changed life; directed and controlled by the Holy Spirit.
6. **James 4:7 – *Humility***: Submits to God's will for his/her life.

_____

_____

_____

_____

_____

_____

_____

_____

Discussion

i.   When Paul used the human body to describe the gifts of the Sprit, why do you think he chose this comparison?

ii. How did he say we should treat those gifts, which are not as prominent as others are, again in comparison to the human body?

iii. How does one gift, differs from the other?

iv. How can the gifts work together for unity?

v.   According to the lesson, how should members treat each other?

vi. How important are the spiritual gifts to the church?

vii. Do you think we need spiritual gifts in this modern age in which we live? Give reasons for your answer.

viii. Why do you think that [**some**] members who hold titles think themselves better than others who are not as educated, or as spiritually gifted?

ix. What did Paul say about the importance of each gift?

Lesson 4: The Gift of the Holy Spirit

John 3:5, Verily, verily, I say unto thee, Except a man be born of water and of the Spirit, he cannot enter into the kingdom of God.

John 14:26, But the Comforter, which is the Holy Ghost, whom the Father will send in my name, he shall teach you all things, and bring all things to your remembrance, whatsoever I have said unto you.

Every gift in the church is a manifestation of the Holy Spirit [**I Corinthians 12:7**]. Therefore, no one can turn the gift on and off when he or she pleases. No one should speak in tongues without the inspiration of the Holy Spirit. He sealed believers at the time of conversion [**Ephesians 1:13**]. Whatever we do in the church of Jesus Christ, must be by the power of the Holy Spirit. He is active in all of our lives, no matter who we are or what gift/s we claim to possess.

Paul pointed out that there are **Diversities of gifts, but the same Spirit. And there are differences of administrations, but the same Lord. And there are diversities of operations, but it is the same God which works all in all** [I Corinthians 12:4-6].

He noted, **All these work that one and the same Spirit, dividing to every man severally as he will** [I **Corinthians 12:11**]. Every gift works together with each other because individually and collectively, they all work with and through the power of the Holy Spirit. It is not for us to direct the Holy Spirit, but for us to listen to Him, and remain obedient to the word of God. The Holy Spirit <u>designs</u>, <u>empowers</u>, and <u>administers</u> each gift accordingly as He chooses.

The Purpose and Function of the Holy Spirit

The Holy Spirit is our Comforter whom Jesus sent to the earth when He returned to His Father in heaven [**John 14:16-17**]. He is <u>guide</u> and <u>teacher</u> who <u>directs</u> and <u>instructs</u> us in the way we should go. He is vital to the life of the Christian who cannot survive without Him. He is the one who <u>inspires</u> us to seek the face of God and to live a life acceptable unto Him.

The Holy Spirit has been involved in all of our lives since the world began. In **Genesis 1:2-3**, we read **And the earth was without form, and void, and darkness was upon the face of the deep. [2]**

And the Spirit of God moved upon the face of the waters. And God said, 'Let there be light:' and there was light. [3]

Distinguishing Features of the Holy Spirit

He was present at creation [**Genesis 1:2**].

He is the author of the Scriptures [**II Samuel 23:2, II Timothy 3:16, II Peter 1:20**].

He was present at the birth of Jesus Christ [**Luke 1:35**].

He is the Comforter, Helper or Paraclete [**John 14:16, 26**].

He is present at our New Birth [**John 3:5**].

He makes intercession for us in prayer [**Romans 8:26**].

He can be grieved [**Ephesians 4:30-31**].

The work of the Holy Spirit is vast and of great significance to the Believer.

Grieving the Holy Spirit

We grieve the Holy Spirit if our lives do not reflect the qualities and requirements of who a Christian ought to be [**Ephesians 4:30-31**]. Therefore, we cannot expect to live a double life with the expectation that the Spirit of God will accept such behaviour. Every one of us must live a life of sanctification, being set apart for God's purpose [**Colossians 3:5, Galatians 5:16, 22-24, Romans 12:1-2, Thessalonians 2:4**].

Baptism in the Holy Spirit

While man baptizes in water, Jesus is the One who baptizes in the Holy Spirit [**John 15:26, Luke 24:49, Acts 1:4-8**]. Baptism in the Holy Spirit is the transforming power that changes us and makes us new people. He gives us a new nature with desires to please God and obey His commandments. Nevertheless, you must believe the changing power of the Holy Spirit. Jesus said, **He that believes and is baptized shall be saved; but he that believes not shall be damned** [Mark 16:16].

The Holy Spirit's Presence

1. He is the *third person* in the godhead [**I John 5:7**]
2. He is *resident* in the life of the believer after receiving Jesus Christ in the heart [**Acts 1:8, Romans 8:11**].
3. He is the one who brings *conviction* to the sinner leading to repentance [**Acts 2:38**].
4. He *adopts* us into the Family of God [**Romans 8:15**].
5. He *seals* us for eternity [**Ephesians 1:13**].
6. He *frees* us from the power of the flesh [**Romans 8:1-2**].
7. He *helps* us in our prayer [**Romans 8:26**].
8. He *intercedes* for us [**Romans 8:27**].
9. He is a *teacher, comforter,* and *guide* [**John 14:26**].
10. He helps us in *sanctification* so that we live in holiness with the Lord [**I Thessalonians**].
11. He brings us into *relationship* with the Father and the Lord Jesus Christ [**John 14:43**].

Spiritual Gifts for the Church

Reflections

1. What do you understand by spiritual gifts? What makes them spiritual when compared to natural gifts, technical or intellectual gifts – those who train for example, to be a mechanic, or doctor?
2. Do you have a gift in which you minister?
3. Does your church encourage the manifestation of the gifts?
4. If you were forbidden to use your gift in the local church, what would you do?
5. How do the spiritual gifts compare with the human body? Why do you think Paul used this illustration?
6. How important is the Holy Spirit to the life of the believer?

Suggestions for further reading

a. John 14:26
b. John 15:26
c. John 16:13
d. Acts 1:5-8
e. Acts 2
f. Acts 6:3
g. Acts 7:54-58
h. Romans 12:6-8
i. I Corinthians 6
j. I Corinthian 12
k. Ephesians 4:11-12
l. II Thessalonians 2:13-17
m. I Peter 1:15-16

Section 3
Spiritual Growth

I believe we have all met people who profess to have been saved for many years, yet they seem so immature and extremely worldly. Some are unruly and use the Holy Spirit as a tool or equipment to turn on and off, as they desire. They speak in tongues at will, which only shows that they are the ones in control. Nevertheless, the word teaches us to **Grow in grace, and in the knowledge of our Lord and Saviour Jesus Christ. To him be glory both now and for ever. Amen** [II Peter 23:18]. This section covers areas such as *Developing in Christ, Fruitfulness, and Faith*.

Developing in Christ
  a. Introduction
  b. Unity of the Faith
  c. Knowledge of Christ
  d. Instability
  e. Truthfulness
  f. Standing Firm Against Heresy

Fruitfulness
  a. Introduction
  b. The True Vine
  c. Evidence of Fruitfulness
  d. Effectiveness
  e. Progressiveness
  f. Productiveness
  g. Virtue

Faith
  a. What is Faith?
  b. Faith in God
  c. Active *and* Dead Faith

Spiritual Growth

Developing in Christ

Ephesians 4:13-16, Colossians 1:9

Introduction

The local church has members from all kinds of spiritual and cultural backgrounds. What is most disturbing are the ones who should be advanced in their Christian experience, yet they are still in spiritual infancy; seemingly, they are spiritually challenged. In my walk, I have met *thieves*, the *contentious*, *deceivers, adulterers, liars*. I mean, outright downright, liars. You may wonder, "How could this be true?" It is a good question, but true. In the church today, some of the members [so-called] are only padding [tares]. They make up the population – membership for various reasons, which in many cases are selfish, and only serve to please and satisfy a spiritually blind or a corrupt leader.

This section will discuss the two passages below.

[**Ephesians 4:13-16**] gives **four important themes** concerning maturity in Christ

  a. *Unity of the faith*: for oneness and effective communication [**13a, 16**]

  b. *Knowledge of Jesus Christ*: for perfection and growth [**13b**];

  c. *Instability*: which prevents maturity [**14**];

  d. *Truthfulness*: integrity for spiritual effectiveness and witnessing [**15**]

Colossians 1:9, there are three factors to help us avoid heresies

  i.   To be filled with all ***knowledge [9]***

  ii. To be filled with all ***wisdom, [9]*** and

  iii. To be filled with spiritual ***understanding[9]***

_____
_____
_____
_____
_____
_____

Lesson 1: Unity of the Faith

Psalm 133, I Corinthians 12:12-20, Ephesians 4:3-5

Introduction

I Corinthians 12:12-14, 18-20

For as the body is one, and hath many members, and all the members of that one body, being many, are one body: so also is Christ. [12]

For by one Spirit are we all baptized into one body, whether we be Jews or Gentiles, whether we be bond or free; and have been all made to drink into one Spirit. [13]

For the body is not one member, but many. [14]

But now hath God set the members every one of them in the body, as it hath pleased him. [18]

And if they were all one member, where (*were*) the body? [19]

But now are they many members, yet but one body. [20]

Ephesians 4:13a, till we all come in the unity of the faith.

If we remain attached to the Lord Jesus Christ, unity will prevail among us as we [**Endeavour to keep the unity of the Spirit in the bond of peace, Ephesians 4:3**]. We must make every effort to maintain peace and harmony among us. When strife and disputes occur: they often spring from legalism, covetousness, interpersonal differences, impatience, and doctrinal interpretation of the Scriptures.

Acts 15:1, And certain men which came down from Judaea taught the brethren, and said, Except ye be circumcised after the manner of Moses, ye cannot be saved. This is an example concerning division and strife in the early church community. There is always someone with a new vision or interpretation of the Scriptures. Another important point is that **legalism** will affect the growth of the church.

A few years ago, I heard of **re-baptism** stating that baptism in <u>Jesus Name</u> is wrong: while another group was teaching that baptism in <u>Father, Son, and Holy Ghost</u> is wrong. These are some of the situations, which cause disputes resulting in disunity and division in the Body of Jesus Christ. In spite of the situation in the early church, through the <u>wisdom</u> and <u>direction</u> of the Holy Spirit, they resolved the dispute by collective discussion [**Read Acts 15**].

2.

Nevertheless, we cannot avoid the development of conflict because it is a way of life. However, when this occurs everyone should aim for a peaceful outcome. If there is competitiveness and jealousies, these will only create more problems and cause setbacks in the body

There will always be unruly people, who will come into the midst as instruments and agents of the enemy. It is important for the leader to be wary of them since those persons will disrupt the mission and plans for the church. They cause discord and chaos. Therefore, Paul admonish the leader thus, **Now I beseech you, brethren, mark them which cause divisions and offenses contrary to the doctrine which ye have learned; and avoid them [Romans 16:17].**

We must work together to be effective in order to edify one another in love. Unity means that we will love each other enough to seek the good of the other. There is harmony, agreement, and accord. We will not **always** see things the same way, but we must love one another, be sensitive, and kind towards each other to maintain the spirit of unity.

Although we live in a broken world, in the church there are certain positive behaviours that should be common among the members.

Paul stated, **Whether one member suffer, all the members suffer with it; or one member be honoured, all the members rejoice with it [I Corinthians 12:26].** This is a demonstration of spiritual unity mentioned in **Ephesians 4:3.** It states, **Endeavouring to keep the unity of the Spirit in the bond of peace.** The verses following **4-6** are of significant importance for unity in the Body of Christ.

Managing Disputes

Christians should be able to manage disputes in an orderly and dignified manner by following the ethical standards in the word of God. **Matthew 18:15-20**, gives a lucid illustration for the procedure concerning resolving problems.

If thy brother shall trespass against thee, go and tell him his fault between thee and him alone: if he shall hear thee, thou has gained thy brother [Matthew 18:15]. We cannot avoid offences because the Scriptures warned us that they would come.

Luke 17:1-3

**It is impossible but that offences will come: but woe unto him through whom they come! [1]
It were better for him that a millstone were hanged about his neck, and he cast into the sea, than that he should offend one of these little ones. [2]
Take heed to yourselves: If thy brother trespass against thee, rebuke him; and if he repent, forgive him. [3]
And if he trespass against thee seven times in a day, and seven times in a day turn again to thee, saying, I repent; thou shalt forgive him. [4]**

> **Rebuke:** *yakhach*, to reason, reprove, correct, and mediate.

Christian Ethics
Galatians 6:1-2

Brethren, if a man be overtaken in a fault, ye which are spiritual, restore such an one in the spirit of meekness; considering thyself, lest thou also be tempted. [1]
Bear ye one another's burdens, and so fulfill the law of Christ. [2]

Overtaken to be caught in a sin.
Fault: a sin involving guilt and generally refers to all sin, unknown and unintentional.
Considering thyself: give attention to yourself lest you fall into the same position.
To fulfill: very full to perfection.
The law of Christ: to love one another.

Restore relationship in the Body of Christ

i. *Restore*: to repair, to make right, adjust and put in the appropriate place. An offended person in this position will make every effort to help the offender and release him or her from guilt.

ii. *Meekness*: This means when the offended goes to the offender he or she will have self-control, being even-tempered, tranquil, and patient; and not use pride or arrogance.

iii. *Tempted*: in this context tempted means to lead someone into sin. It also speaks of the trying of your faith; your strength; disposition; patience and character in settling a dispute. We must always keep in mind that anyone can fall into sin because the tempter is ever on our path to distract and allure us. In essence, we will be tested at some time or another. Our response will prove who we are, and who is governing our life.

There are two vital elements, which we need for spiritual growth to be effective and they are prayer and regular participation in the Holy Communion.

Prayer

No Christian can survive without having a consistent prayer life. Jesus was our greatest example for leading a life of prayer before His disciples, which made them ask Him to teach them to pray [**Luke 11:1**]. Immediately, Jesus responded to their request, and taught them the art of praying [**Luke 11:2-4, Matthew 6:9-11, and 7:7-11**].
Prayer is essential to the Christian as oxygen is to life. Paul encouraged the believer to

Prayer: *proseúchomai,* the act of praying to God either for obtaining good, or to avert evil. It is also for giving thanks, asking, or requesting special things.

Continue in prayer, and watch in the same with thanksgiving;
[Colossians 4:3]. Pray without ceasing [I Thessalonians 5:17].

The Holy Communion

It is important that every believer regularly partake of the Holy Communion to draw closer to the Lord and to grow in Him. Jesus said, **Take eat: this is my body, which is broken for you: this do in remembrance of me. This cup is the new testament in my blood: this do ye, as of as ye drink *it*, in remembrance of me, [Matthew 26:24-25].**

When Jesus said **this do in remembrance of me,** He does not want us to forget the great price He paid for our redemption on Calvary's Cross. Therefore, we should not take it lightly when we come to the communion table. It should be a place where as Paul said, we tarry one for the other. It is also important that we do not participate in doubt or unbelief; but trust in the Lord for our cleansing, recognizing that the blood cleanses us from all sins.

Suggestions for further reading

a.   Leviticus 19:16-18
b.   Matthew 18:15-20
c.   Matthew 26:26ff
d.   Matthew 7:7-11
e.   I Corinthians 11:24-33
f.   Galatians 6:1-2

Discussion

a.   Why do you think Christians hold on to grudges?
b.   Do you believe that when someone offends you, you should be the one to make right?
c.   What would you do if the individual refuses to agree with you? What should be your next move?
d.   How would you deal with someone who wants to involve you into sin?
e.   Should you blame an individual who entices you to sin?

Lesson 2: Knowledge of Jesus Christ

Galatians 5:1, 13-16, Colossians 2, I John 2:7-14, 4:7-21

Introduction

Ephesians 4:13b, And of the knowledge of the Son of God, unto a perfect man, unto the measure of the stature of the fullness of Christ.

Colossians 2:8, Beware lest any man spoil you through philosophy and vain deceit, after the tradition of men, after the rudiments of the world, and not after Christ.

> **Rudiments:** basic worldly principles and ideologies. Teachings differing from the spiritual doctrines of Christ.

The salient concepts in **Ephesians 4:13b**, points out **knowledge**: expertise; being **perfect**: completeness: **measure**: quantity; **stature**: prominence, and **fullness**: richness. We must understand who Jesus is and what He stands for before we can represent Him. For any relationship to grow, each person must know about the other concerning what is acceptable, and what is not. Our relationship with Jesus Christ brings us into personal understanding of Him.

Relationship with the Lord Jesus Christ

When we have an intimate relationship with Jesus Christ, it enables us to live a life pleasing to Him ethically, morally, spiritually, and emotionally. These factors set us apart as children of God. Moreover, it is our relationship with Him, which will motivate us to aim for growth in order to develop spiritual dimensions in height, depth, and width.

It is knowledge of the Lord Jesus, which will make us love one another as He asked us to do. As we continue to know the Lord and develop His character, our walk becomes stronger in Him, and we are more confident as we dedicate our lives to Him. We live in unity with one another, thus preventing the spirit of division, which will cause strife.

Moreover, experiencing the fullness of Jesus Christ means total abandonment to His will [**Luke 9:23**]. We must measure up to His standard, which leads to a life satiated with His grace, and completely turned over to His will. Clearly, to measure up means we *speak* like Him, *walk* like Him, *behave* and *live* like Him. Our character will be Christ-like, separated from worldly lusts, desires, and attractions. *Is this possible*?

Yes, with God all things are possible [**Luke 1:37, But with God, nothing shall be impossible**]. If we believe these words, then we know that anything is possible when we put our trust in God.

To help us develop true understanding of Jesus Christ we must identify and deal with weaknesses in our personal lives. We must check our armour each day for kinks and areas, which will cause the enemy to enter and sabotage our plans.

Love for each Other

Our knowledge of Jesus Christ will make us love each other [**II John 4-6**]. When we have personal knowledge of Jesus Christ, we will seek for unity in the Body to maintain perfection that will benefit all believers. As we compare our lives to Jesus Christ, the Holy Spirit will detect weaknesses and help us bring these to the Lord in prayer [**Romans 8:26**]. If we examine ourselves each day, we will know open doors of hatred and malice, which will cause the enemy to gain entry into our lives, and this, will defeat our purpose of serving the Lord in true holiness. It is our love for each other, which will influence others to want to know the Lord. Furthermore, it is our knowledge of Jesus Christ that will determine the kind of life we manifest to the world that will attract others to Him [**Matthew 5:16**].

Suggestions for further reading

a. Colossians 2
b. I Peter 1
c. II Peter 2
d. II Peter 3:18

Discussion

i.   Since the Holy Spirit is a teacher and knows all things, why should be seek further knowledge of Jesus Christ?

ii. What purpose will knowledge of Jesus Christ serve in the life of the believer?

iii. How can we show that we know Jesus Christ?

iv. How do we go about knowing the Lord Jesus Christ?

_____
_____
_____
_____
_____
_____
_____
_____
_____
_____
_____

Lesson 3: Instability

Read II Timothy 3:1-9

Introduction

That we henceforth be no more children, tossed to and fro, and carried about with every wind of doctrine, by the sleight of men, and cunning craftiness, whereby they lie in wait to deceive [Ephesians 4:14].

> **Sleight:** fraud, trickery

The unstable Christian is easily led by all kinds of forces within and without, and by the imaginations of the mind. From the verse above, we can elicit the following **five** points:

a. *children tossed to and fro*

b. *every wind of doctrine*

c. *sleight of men* — Fraud trickery

d. *cunning craftiness*

e. *lie in wait to deceive*

Children tossed to and fro

The Christian population in any local church consists of a multi-religious group coming from a variety of denominations, and spiritual experiences. Each person has a different concept of Christianity, and for this reason; there are many conflicts and dissatisfaction among groups. Occasionally, the reason for this mixed multitude comes from the search for "the perfect church," which does not exist here on earth. Next, for many there is lack of integrity, narcissism, and demonic possession.

A typical feature of the unstable individual is double-mindedness. It means he or she is unable to make decisions based on personal values and principles. Instead, the individual will support anyone at any time depending on the social or doctrinal climatic conditions, and for personal satisfaction. There is no desire for integrity, loyalty, or faithfulness. Those persons are easily led astray by anyone who speaks desirable words at the right time.

Furthermore, there is no allegiance to any particular leader, religion, or group. Is it any wonder that Paul described those persons as being tossed **to and fro**. One could further describe the unstable person as the chaff which the wind drives away [**Psalm 1:4**]. They have no strength, but are weak and fragile. Therefore, they respond to any thing; and will follow anyone.

To be **tossed to and fro**, refers to restlessness, instability, discontent, unreliability and such like. There is no depth, purpose or true desire to learn or spending time to know the Lord. We can only be perfect when we give ourselves to loyal faithful service to the Lord in absolute obedience. God expects reliability and commitment in serving Him.

The Christian life must not be relative when it comes to our relationship with Jesus Christ. Instead, it must be absolute with the help of the indwelling Holy Spirit.

The loyal Christian does not give way to worldly standards for living. Instead, dependence is upon the Holy Spirit. When we accept the Lord Jesus Christ in our lives, we must grow and develop in the faith. We must show maturity by the fruits we produce. Our lives must be different from those who do not know Jesus Christ. To grow in the Lord means we must cast off attitudes and behaviours, which are contrary to our relationship with him and His will for us.

Every Wind of Doctrine

II Timothy 3:7-9

Ever learning, and never able to come to the knowledge of the truth. [7]

Now as Jannes and Jambres withstood Moses, so do these also resist the truth: men of corrupt minds, reprobate concerning the faith. [8]

But they shall proceed no further: for their folly shall be manifest unto all (*men*), as theirs also was. [9]

Since the unstable Christian is insincere, he or she will accept teachings, which comply with the desires of the heart and needs. According to Paul, they are **Ever learning, and never able to come to the knowledge of the truth,** [**II Timothy 3:7**]. Notice, they are ever learning, but never able to come to the knowledge of the truth.

Apparently, there is nothing that can be done for those persons, because they are always opposing the truth of God's word. They interpret the Scriptures for their own pleasures and desires. They can be a great burden in any church organization, and an obstacle in the path of the mission.

This kind of behaviour does not refer only to the church member, but also to leaders who reject the teachings of the Apostles and the leading of the Holy Spirit. They defy even the working of the Holy Spirit in the midst of their gatherings. Obviously, they are open to all kinds of doctrines.

Paul did not stop at **verse 7**, but compared them to those who opposed Moses [**8**], and showed the disastrous end of their behaviour [**9**]. Undoubtedly, those who oppose the word of God will reap their reward in due time.

The Sleight of men

Today we hear of all kinds of trickery used by some leaders in order to gain popularity, and financial power. For the most part, at any time, one can turn on a Christian television program and the individual will *preface*, *interject*, or *conclude* with the request for an offering. He will make promises of healing and deliverance, and so on only to get into someone's pocket. They use all kinds of gimmicks to get their act across to the vulnerable and those who are unstable.

Cunning Craftiness

Seemingly, the calculating scammer has left the outside world to infiltrate the church community. The spirits of greed and selfishness have become the order of the day. Some preface their entrance with their popularity, and not with the full gospel of Jesus Christ. The Holy Spirit's evidence is a holler, scream, and loud music.

Lie in wait to Deceive

For they that are such serve not our Lord Jesus Christ, but their own belly; and by good words and fair speeches deceive the hearts of the simple, [Romans 16:18].

This verse climax **Ephesians 4:14**. It gives a clear understanding of what Paul was talking about and the description of false teachers. Indeed, those unscrupulous persons who pose themselves to be Christians serve their own selves and not the people of God. They use words, which are acceptable by society and those who are comfortable in their sins. They do not want to hear the truths of God's word, but rather accept deception because it makes them feel good. Those persons do not have to concern themselves about holiness.

Inconsistency in the Faith [James 1:5-8, II Timothy 3:2-5]

The unstable Christian is easily led astray by all kinds of forces. Children are impressionable, and easily influenced by distractions, because they are not yet grown, and do not have experience about coping with problems. Therefore, they believe anything and accept anything they are told. Likewise, the unstable Christian who does not take time to know Jesus Christ through the word and disciplines of prayer and fasting, will be misled into any false doctrine given by false teachers. The unstable individual will be misled by the sleight of cunning men who use fraudulent speech to re-direct them from the faith [**Romans 16:18**].

The Open Door

The unstable believer leaves the door open for the enemy to gain entrance into his life to use him as an instrument for sin. Paul noted that we should not *...***give place to the devil, [Ephesians 4:27]**. The devil is our adversary, who behaves like a roaring lion. His aim is to devour those who are careless and live ungodly lives. Peter encourages believers to steadfastly [*persistently, consistently, constantly*] resist the devil.

[I Peter 5:8-9], Be sober, be vigilant; because your adversary the devil, as a roaring lion, walks about, seeking whom he may devour: [8]

Whom resist steadfast in the faith, knowing that the same afflictions are accomplished in your brethren that are in the world]. [9]

Lack of Spiritual Growth

Jesus spoke of the <u>sower</u>, the <u>seeds</u>, and different types of <u>soil</u> in **Luke 8:4-15**. The text teaches about the circumstances in which the seeds fell.

i. Careless Believers [way side seeds]

Some fell by the way side; and was trodden down, and the fowls of the air devoured it. [5]

Those by the way side are they that hear; then comes the devil, and takes away the word out of their hearts, lest they should believe and be saved [12].

This reflects carelessness and lack of interest in the things of God. They allow the devil to entice them and to snatch the word of truth out of their hearts.

ii. Unfaithful Believers [seeds on the rock]

And some fell upon a rock; and as soon as it was sprung up, it withered away, because it lacked moisture. [6]

They on the rock are they, which, when they hear, receive the word with joy; and these have no root, which for a while believe, and in time of temptation fall away [13].

So many people walk down a church aisle to receive the Lord Jesus Christ. After this initiation, some went directly into the ministry because they were told that they had the gift for pastoring. Nevertheless, they soon gave up when hardships, trials and tests come their way. They quickly fold up their tent and walk away. The reason is that there is no growth and experience in reading, understanding, and applying the word of God. It was all a moment of excitement, but nothing on the inside to hold that person together.

iii. Church-goers: Unstable Worldly Believers [those among thorns]

Some fell among thorns; and the thorns sprang up with it, and choked it [7]

And they that fell among thorns are they, which, when they heard, go forth, and are choked with cares and riches and pleasures of this life, and bring no fruit to perfection. [14]

> **Care**: *merimna*, distractions, anxieties, burdens, and worries. Being anxious about everyday things rather than trust in God. [*See Philippians 4:6-8*].
> **Perfection**: *maturity*

There are people who are not willing to change from the old lifestyle. They believe they can serve God and the devil simultaneously: *impossible*! The believer who remains in a state of instability will not grow and mature, but remains in spiritual infancy, still drinking milk. This situation causes frustration due to lack of spiritual disciplines and character. Those persons in this category are simply church-goers who have no real relationship with the Lord Jesus Christ. They know of Jesus, but do not know Him, they are ever learning with no power [**II Timothy 3:1-9**].

iv. *Faithful Believers*: reliable, trustworthy, patient, sincere [good ground]

And other fell on good ground, and sprang up, and bear fruit an hundred-fold. [8a]

But that on the good ground are they, which in an honest and good heart, having heard the word, keep it, and bring forth fruit with patience. [15]

> **An honest and good heart:** a *noble* heart
> **Patience:** *hupomone*, constancy, perseverance, steadfastness. Being able to cope even under difficult and severe situations, yet still trusting, with hopefulness.

There is hardly any need for improvement on these two verses. If you are faithfully serving the Lord, then you are good soil. It means that you are growing, and bearing fruit. According to Jesus, if you do not abide in Him, you cannot bear fruit [**John 15:1-7**].

_____

_____

_____

_____

_____

_____

_____

_____

_____

_____

_____

_____

_____

_____

_____

_____

_____

_____

_____

_____

_____

_____

_____

_____
_____
_____
_____
_____
_____
_____
_____
_____
_____
_____
_____
_____
_____
_____
_____
_____
_____
_____
_____
_____
_____
_____
_____
_____
_____
_____
_____
_____
_____
_____
_____
_____
_____

Lesson 4: Truthfulness

Zechariah 8:16-7, Ephesians 4:15

Introduction

Ephesians 4:15

But speaking the truth in love, may grow up into him in all things, which is the heard, even Christ.

Zechariah 8:16-17

Speak ye every man the truth to his neighbour; execute the judgment of truth and peace in your gates: [16]

And let none of you imagine evil in your hearts against his neighbour; and love no false oath: for all these are [things] that I hate, saith the Lord. [17]

Speaking the Truth in Love

To speak the truth in love includes positive behaviour, sensitivity, conduct, effective interaction with others, interpersonal relationship, and communication. They are the qualities among others that will truly show who we are and express what we believe. It also refers to spiritual integrity, which sets us apart from those who are insincere and dishonest.

The characteristics of every Christian should be honesty and integrity. When each one respects the other and there is a close connection with the Lord, we will do things that will bring unity and produce fruits of holiness.

Everyone must endeavour to show love with sincerity and transparency without hidden agendas. This requires faithfulness, loyalty and uprightness. Your word must be your bond.

Truthfulness also includes living a life with distinct qualities depicting a true child of God. It must be the norm and not incidental.

God loves us not because we are good, but because we need help. It was not what man desired, but what was best for him. Therefore, we should love each other with truthfulness, honesty, and faithfulness.

Spiritual Integrity

When we practice integrity, there will be positive growth in the knowledge of Christ, with understanding, and wisdom. We learn, develop, grow, and mature when we acknowledge that Jesus Christ is Lord of our lives. He is the head of the church [the Body] and all members, individually is attached to Him [**John 15:1-7**].

Be Attached to the True Vine

John 15:1-7

I am the true vine, and my Father is the husbandman. [1]

Every branch in me that bears not fruit he takes away: and every branch that bears fruit, he purges it that it may bring forth more fruit. [2]

Now ye are clean through the word which I have spoken unto you. [3]

Abide in me, and I in you. As the branch cannot bear fruit of itself, except it abide in the vine; no more can ye, except ye abide in me. [4]

I am the vine, ye are the branches: He that abides in me, and I in him, the same brings forth much fruit: for without me ye can do nothing. [5]

If any man abides not in me, he is cast forth as a branch, and is withered; and men gather them, and cast them into the fire, and they are burned. [6]

If ye abide in me, and my words abide in you, ye shall ask what ye will, and it shall be done unto you. [7]

True: *alēthinós*, real, genuine.
Purge: *kathaíro*, to clean, without stain or spot. To purify.
Abide: *méno*, to stand firm or steadfast.

Discussion

i. If you received Jesus Christ in your heart, why should you be purged?

ii. What do you think Jesus meant when He said, **For without me, ye can do nothing**?

iii. What do you need to do to bear more fruit?

iv. If you do not think you are bearing fruit, what changes do you need to make in your life?

v. Can you describe some of the fruits Christians should produce?

vi. What does it means to be attached to the vine?

vii. Why do you think Jesus called himself The True Vine?

_____
_____
_____
_____
_____
_____
_____
_____
_____
_____

_____

_____

_____

_____

_____

_____

_____

_____

_____

_____

_____

_____

_____

_____

_____

_____

_____

_____

_____

_____

_____

_____

_____

_____

_____

_____

_____

_____

_____

_____

_____

_____

_____

_____

_____

_____

_____

_____

_____

_____

Colosse

The city of Colosse was located in Asia Minor east of Ephesus. One of the persons mentioned in Colossians was Epaphras who seemed to have been active in this church and apparently an associate of Paul. These early Colossian Christians were facing various new ideologies brought to them by heretics who promised them a new way of thinking. This was contrary to the doctrine taught to them by Paul.

Apparently, Paul heard about this situation and while he was in prison, he wrote this epistle to encourage the Colossians that Christ is all they need, and to stabilize their faith in Him. His aim was to divert them from the false philosophies, which seemed to blend new pluralistic beliefs of religion and other practices. Those new believers would undoubtedly have been confused trying to put the two beliefs together.

Paul showed them that the doctrine of Christ is absolute and cannot be mixed with anything else. They are complete in Him and need nothing more to enhance what he taught to them [**See Colossians 2:9-10**]. He showed them that the new theory was heresy, and they should not return to paganism, which does not lead to a saving knowledge of Jesus Christ.

In this epistle, he showed them Jesus' pre-eminence over all; **And that He is before all things, and by him all things consist [Colossians 1:17]**.

_____
_____
_____
_____
_____
_____
_____
_____
_____
_____
_____
_____
_____

Dissent from Accepted or dominant Opinion.

Heresy — an opinion or doctrine in conflict with orthodox religious beliefs

Heretic: A dissenter from orthodox beliefs

Orthodox: Adhereing to established or traditional beliefs.

Lesson 5: Standing Firm *against* Heresy

Colossians 1:9-17

Introduction

Colossians 1:9-17

In the early church, there were all kinds of heresies to deceive the minds of the new Christians. Here Paul is encouraging the believers stating,

For this cause we also, since the day we heard it, do not cease to pray for you, and to desire that ye might be filled with the knowledge of his will in all wisdom and spiritual understanding; [9]

That ye might walk worthy of the Lord unto all pleasing, being fruitful in every good work, and increasing in the knowledge of God; [10]

Strengthened with all might, according to his glorious power, unto all patience and longsuffering with joyfulness; [11]

Giving thanks unto the Father, which hath made us meet to be partakers of the inheritance of the saints in light: [12]

Who hath delivered us from the power of darkness, and hath translated us into the kingdom of his dear Son: [13]

In whom we have redemption through the blood, even the forgiveness of sins: [14]

Who is the image of the invisible God, the firstborn of every creature: [15]

For by him were all things created, that are in heaven, and that in the earth, visible and invisible, whether they be thrones, or dominions, or principalities, or powers: all things were created by him, and for him: [16]

And he is before all things, and by him all things consist. [17]

This is the longest sentence I recall ever reading in the Bible. It explains and brings to light the Person of Jesus Christ, and encourages believers who believe in Him to stay on course. It encourages believers to stand firm with Jesus, and not to stray into heresy. The passage speaks of *edification* through knowledge, wisdom, and spiritual understanding.

To be filled with Knowledge

Since the aim of those who are deceivers is to bring new knowledge to the simple, Paul was instructing the Colossians not to heed the new doctrines of the heretics, but rather to filled with the knowledge of Jesus Christ. Those persons were deceivers who had a form of doctrine, but denied the truth and the power of God. He <u>encouraged</u> them to continue in their faithfulness to God, and not to deviate to anything new. In contrast, Paul <u>commended</u> them for their **faith in Christ Jesus, and their love for the saints** [Colossians 1:4].

Clearly, the only way we will grow and develop in Christ, is to remain faithful to Him in obedience and service. We must not allow modern **doctrines**, which are <u>distorted</u> and <u>worldly</u> to dominate and direct our lives.

Do not be intimidated by someone who will bring some new prophecy to trick you. Read the <u>word of God</u>, attend <u>Bible Study</u>, Sundays or in the week, attend <u>prayer meeting</u> and keep in <u>connection with the people of God</u>. Heretics feed their ego, with nothing new to give to the Body of Christ.

What is Knowledge?
[Colossians 1:9]

For this cause we also, since the day we heard it, do not cease to pray for you, and to desire that ye might be filled with the knowledge of his will in all wisdom and spiritual understanding.

Knowledge here means to have the right information and facts in order to perform what is required of us by the Lord. We will immerse ourselves in study to gain the understanding and knowledge we need to help us mature in faith to stand firmly in Christ.

Spiritual knowledge gives us power and influence over the enemy, preventing us from following after heretics. A thorough and comprehensive understanding of Jesus Christ will enable us to maintain integrity, as we grow in our Christian walk.

If we do not take time to know the Lord, <u>we cannot live for him</u>, <u>we will not trust Him</u>, and <u>we will not seek to please Him</u> because we would not know how to do this. Therefore, experience in learning about the Lord is vital for spiritual growth.

1. We know the Lord by *reading, understanding, and applying his word to our life*
2. We know him by *spending time in prayer*
3. We know Him through *church attendance with other believers*
4. Knowledge of the *Lord brings awareness to what He requires of us*

_____

_____

_____

To be filled with all Wisdom

Wisdom is having knowledge and unique insight about how to deal with a matter. It is perception of what is happening and how to use good judgment to clarify and settle things, which trouble us. It is being able to use knowledge precisely and to control emotions. Nevertheless, wisdom comes directly from God through the Holy Spirit. God will give wisdom to anyone who asks in faith.

Knowledge of God's word is important, but we must also know how to use His word. James advises us that, **if any of you lack wisdom, let him ask of God, that gives to all men liberally, and upbraids not, and it shall be given him, [James 1:5].**

No child of God needs to live in ignorance due to lack of knowledge of God's word, and full understanding about how to apply it. Further, no child of God should live without wisdom when God is willing to give to each one who asks. Moreover, God's wisdom is <u>pure</u>, <u>peaceable</u>, <u>gentle</u>, and <u>full of mercy</u> [**James 3:17, But the wisdom that is from above is first pure, then peaceable, gentle, and easy to be entreated, full of mercy and good fruits, without partiality, and without hypocrisy**].

Wisdom can be in the practical sense for <u>skills</u> and <u>resolving disputes</u>. With spiritual wisdom, this gives us the right application of knowledge, and insight into the true nature of things. Wisdom will guide and direct us in the right way to go.

We need wisdom when witnessing for the Lord in order to choose the right approach and the right time. [**Colossians 4:5, Walk in wisdom toward them that are without, redeeming the time**]. The believer is always in the face of the world where every error is noted and passed on to the enter Body. It is important to understand that we cannot work effectively without the wisdom of God's word.

Knowing His word gives us power through the Holy Spirit who teaches us what to do and when to do what we are given. Keep in mind that without the Holy Spirit, we can do nothing. The gifts we receive, we must have wisdom to know how to use them, and above all, involve the Holy Spirit in every decision we make. We must let Him be our guide and advisor [**Proverbs 3:5-6**].

To be filled with Spiritual Understanding

What is spiritual understanding? It means that you have perception of what the Holy Spirit is saying concerning what He requires of you. As a spiritual person in the practical sense, you are sympathetic and considerate about the feelings of others. Therefore, you will not willfully cause hurt because you are aware of the embarrassment it would cause. When we walk in the Spirit, we will be sensitive to another person's feelings and we will seek to please God rather than our flesh. [**Galatians 5:16, Walk in the Spirit, and ye shall not fulfill the lust of the flesh**].

In addition, spiritual understanding means having knowledge about something maybe through discernment or learning. Next, you need to know how to use that knowledge, and this is where wisdom comes in.

Discussion

i.   Why do you think leaders should be very concerned about the persons they invite to the church to preach to their people?

ii.   How can God's people be led astray by heresies?

iii.   In what ways do you think that there are people who are listening to false doctrines, when the Bible has the answers for their need?

iv.   Do you believe that all the versions of the Bible available today are the true unadulterated word of God?

v.   What was the purpose for keeping the Colossians on the right path so that they did not return to paganism?

vi.   What are some reasons why people would go astray and return to false doctrines?

vii.   What should believers do to stay in the will of God to avoid being led astray by false doctrines?

Lesson 6: Fruitfulness

II Peter 1:1-10, John 15:1-7

Introduction

Every Christian ought to show signs of <u>growth</u> and <u>maturity</u> by the fruit he or she produces. There must be evidence of growth, progress and development, which the world can see. It is the life the individual demonstrates to others, which will show a change in the character and behaviour.

The word teaches, **Therefore, if any man be in Christ he is a new creature: old things are passed away: behold, all things are become new, [I Corinthians 5:17].** Obviously, there must be evidence of change and growth.

Additionally, Jesus told us that the branch, which does not bear fruit, must be cut off and put in the fire to be burned. Hence, all believers must bear fruit that will remain **[Galatians 5:22-23, John 15:1-7]**. This speaks of virtue and growth in Christ Jesus. To bear fruit means, the individual stays close to the Lord in obedience, and must be willing to suffer for His cause.

Accordingly Jesus said, **If any man will come after me, let him deny himself, and take up his cross daily, and follow me, [Luke 9:23].**

Fruitfulness refers to facing all kinds of spiritual weather similar to the natural fruit trees. Nevertheless, they remain stable and continue in their function of bearing fruit regardless of the conditions.

_____

_____

_____

_____

_____

_____

_____

_____

_____

_____

Encouragement to be a Virtuous Christian

II Peter 1:3-10

According as his divine power hath given unto us all things that pertain unto life and godliness, through the knowledge of him that hath called us to glory and virtue: [3]

Whereby are given unto us exceeding great and precious promises: that by these ye might be partakers of the divine nature, having escaped the corruption that is in the world through lust. [4]

And beside this, giving all diligence, add to your faith virtue; and to virtue knowledge; [5]

And to knowledge temperance; and to temperance patience; and to patience godliness; [6]

And to godliness brotherly kindness; and to brotherly kindness charity. [7]

For if these things be in you, and abound, they make you that ye shall neither be barren nor unfruitful in the knowledge of our Lord Jesus Christ. [8]

But he that lacks these things is blind, and cannot see afar off, and hath forgotten that he was purged from his old sins. [9]

Wherefore the rather, brethren, give diligence to make your calling and election sure: for if ye do these things, ye shall never fall: [10]

The entire passage is encouraging the child of God to grow in Christ Jesus. When we become Born Again, there must be evidence of change through the fruits, which we produce. Moreover, Peter is teaching that we must demonstrate behaviours showing the traits of Jesus's character in us.

Virtue means *moral excellence; signifying the intrinsic values* of Christianity found in **Galatians 5:22-23, and other passages**. This means our lives will reveal features, which are different from those of persons who not know the Lord Jesus Christ. We cannot emulate someone we do not know. Therefore, we must have a saving knowledge of Jesus Christ.

We must know what He desires us to be. We must spend time with Him in prayer, meditation, reading and application of the word. Since we were all born in sin with the sinful nature [**Ephesians 2:1-3**], we need a new nature.

In order for us to be virtuous; through **His divine power, God has given us all things that pertain to life and godliness [II Peter 1:3]**. It is through God's power that we will be able to change the old adamic nature of wrath and sinfulness to one of purity, holiness, and grace.

We obtain those blessings because of the great and precious promises, enabling us to partake of the divine nature of God. Peter admonishes that if these virtues are in us, **and abound, we will neither be barren nor unfruitful in the knowledge of our Lord Jesus Christ**.

In contrast, he speaks to those who are careless and worldly; meaning they lack these virtues. Describing them as **blind, and cannot see afar off, and hath forgotten that he was purged from his old sins**.

No one in this situation bears fruits. That person is tossed about by every wind of doctrine with no resting place.

To be fruitful, our lives must be stable for us to learn about the Lord Jesus Christ so that we can bear fruit, which will remain. When a Christian lives by the philosophies and teachings of ungodly people, he or she will fall into temptation to leave the truth of God's word and believe a lie. The virtuous Christian has an active relationship with the Lord seen by those who are around him or her. It is a life of upright, honest, and moral living.

Discussion

i.   Why is it so important for Christians to live virtuous lives?

ii. How is it possible to be virtuous in such a time as which we are living?

iii. How can anyone be virtuous when there is hardly anyone who can be trusted?

iv. What do you think Peter meant when he said, "*According as his divine power hath given unto us all things that pertain unto life and godliness*," yet there are people who are hurting financially and spiritually?

v.   What does being virtuous means?

vi. What do you understand by, "*But he that lacks these things is blind, and cannot see afar off, and hath forgotten that he was purged from his old sins.*"

vii. What do you think Peter meant by "**your calling and election?**"

The True Vine

John 15:1-7

I am the true vine, and my Father is the husbandman. [1]

Every branch in me that bears not fruit he takes away: and every branch that bears fruit, he purges it, that it may bring forth more fruit. [2]

Now ye are clean through the word which I have spoken unto you. [3]

Abide in me, and I in you. As the branch cannot bear fruit of itself, except it abide in the vine: no more can ye, except ye abide in me. [4]

I am the vine, ye are the branches: He that abides in me, and I in him, the same brings forth much fruit: for without me ye can do nothing. [5]

If a man abides not in me, he is cast forth as a branch, and is withered; and men gather them, and cast them into the fire, and they are burned. [6]

If ye abide in me, and my words abide in you, ye shall ask what ye will, and it shall be done unto you. [7]

This passage affirms that we cannot bear fruit unless we are attached to the *True Vine*. It means we cannot live in the flesh and expect to bear spiritual fruit. Jesus said, **Abide in me, and I in you. As the branch cannot bear fruit of itself, except it abide in the vine: no more can ye, except ye abide in me,** [John 15:4]. Any Christian who does not bear fruit is an enemy of the Cross of Christ [**Philippians 3:18**]. Paul further noted that individuals in this position bring sorrow to him. He noted that their **end is destruction, whose God is their belly, and whose glory is in their shame, who mind earthly things** [**Philippians 3:19**]. No one who is unattached to the Vine can bear fruit, which will remain.

To be attached to Jesus Christ means walking in holiness, obedience, and faithfulness. If anyone decides to choose an alternative life in serving the Lord, other than the precepts laid down in the word, that person is an enemy to the Cross of Jesus Christ. Too many are using worldly philosophies and ideologies in an attempt to live for Christ, but it will not work.

According to the word, **I am the vine, ye are the branches: He that abides in me, and I in him, the same brings forth much fruit: for without me ye can do nothing** [**John 15:5**]. Therefore, no other substance or teachings will suffice, unless we all come under the banner of the Cross. We must remain attached to the True Vine in order to bring forth much fruit, and to abide in the will of the Lord.

_____
_____
_____
_____

The Fruit of the Spirit

Galatians 5:22-23

But the fruit of the Spirit is love, joy, peace, longsuffering, gentleness, goodness, faith, [22] Meekness, temperance, against such there is no law. [23]

To be fruitful, we must nourish ourselves with the right substance. Jesus said,

Abide in me, and I in you. As the branch cannot bear fruit of itself, except it abide in the vine: no more can ye, except ye abide in me [John 15:4].

When we remain *attached* to the True Vine, we are in a position to bear the **Fruit of the Spirit**, which will remain and make us strong.

Why is the Fruit of the Spirit so Important to our Christian Walk?

1. Evidence of *Fruit of the Spirit* reflects <u>character</u> in the life of the individual. It means there is <u>discipline</u> in that person's life. There is <u>self-control</u> and <u>confidence</u> because the Holy Spirit controls the life of the individual [**Galatians 5:16**]. There is trust in the Lord, rather than depending on self. Walking in the Spirit means you have **crucified the flesh with the affections and lusts [Galatians 5:24]**.

2. The *Fruit of the Spirit* helps us to <u>communicate</u> with God in order to please Him in spirit and in truth.

3. The *Fruit of the Spirit* helps us in our <u>relationship with others</u>. It helps us to conduct ourselves in a Christian manner, and to control our emotions so that our interpersonal relationships will constantly depict a changed life [**Ephesians 4:32**].

4. The *Fruit of the Spirit* enables us <u>to develop principles</u>, which will guide us to live a life pleasing unto Christ.

_____
_____
_____
_____
_____
_____
_____
_____
_____
_____
_____
_____
_____
_____
_____

Lesson 7: Faith

Romans 4, Hebrews 11

Introduction

What is Faith?

I believe that the moment we hear the word faith, we begin to look at someone or within ourselves. We are searching for something that will give us a fixation on something or someone, even ourselves. It is having a belief about some interest about what you *heard*, *read*, or *saw*, but with no knowledge about.

The Bible teaches that, **Faith is the substance of things hoped for, the evidence of things not seen, [Hebrews 11:1]**. This verse is stating that we have confidence in divine truths, for which we have no logical proof, but we believe.

> **Faith**: *pistis*, confidence, conviction, trust, belief, reliance, trustworthiness, and persuasion.
> **Substance**: *huphistamai*, basis or foundation, confident expectation.
> **Evidence**: *Élegchos*; conviction.

Additionally, the verse means that through **faith**, we are standing under the claim to our conviction, that our expectation will be realized concerning [**things hoped for**].

Our standing under the principles of faith, then, is the **evidence** the world will sees concerning our faith in God. We can accept that, the evidence of faith means more than just having a conviction.

Rather, we must demonstrate the truth of our belief. Otherwise, faith is dead and has no life. We cannot keep faith locked up without expressing what we believe. It is more than a feeling: faith is reality of our conviction about something or someone. Therefore, **faith eliminates** doubt, fear, and unbelief. Consequently, our assurance and confidence rest on God's promises to us.

For example, we believe and accept the origin and **foundation of our salvation**. According to the word, **For by grace are ye saved through faith; and that not of yourselves: it is the gift of God, [Ephesians 2:8]**. Evidently, we cannot accept this truth other than through faith. **This is faith in action**.

_____

_____

_____

_____

Temporal Faith that we show exercise in the car, bus, airplane Chairm we sit in bus that pays wps

Faith in God

Mark 11:22-24

Have faith in God. [22]

For verily I say unto, That whosoever shall say unto this mountain, Be thou removed, and be thou cast into the sea; and shall not doubt in his heart, but shall believe that those things which he saith shall come to pass; he shall have whatsoever he saith. [23]

Therefore, I say unto you, What things soever ye desire, when ye pray, believe that ye receive them, and ye shall have them. [24]

When Jesus referred to "this mountain," He used it only as a symbol concerning obstacles or difficulties, which we often face in our Christian life. He was pointing out that if we have faith [belief, trust, confidence], we can **command** and **expect** changes in our lives.

Moreover, Jesus gave an example of effective faith through believing prayer when He cursed the fig tree [**Mark 11:12-14**]. This does not mean we should go around cursing people or things, which do not comply with our desires. Jesus was making a statement of faith, through belief, and courage.

Jesus wants us to have faith in God, and demonstrated how this is done. He showed that we too, could take authority over a situation, which seems difficult, through passionate, prevailing, effective, fervent prayer [**James 5:16b**]. Jesus showed that we, through faith, have authority in the spiritual realm to bring about things in the natural.

Active *and* Dead Faith

There must be evidence of faith; otherwise, it is either weak or dead. We prove that our faith is alive by our works. According to **James 2:17**, **Even so faith, if it hath not works is dead, being alone**. Moreover, the person of faith will not worry, murmur, or complain. That individual thinks and acts with expectation that prayers will be answered in God's time. Faith requires patience, and James used Abraham as an example of faith in action by his works [**James 2:21-22**].

Living, active faith has no room for doubt and unbelief. It may seem easy to say that "I have faith," but cannot show the evidence of faith if there is doubt. When we exercise faith in God, there must be evidence of that belief. We cannot have faith and unbelief in the same place. It takes faith to bring about the promises of God, and faith becomes perfect when we trust, wait, and expect God's promises.

The Bible teaches, **Without faith, it is impossible to please God**… [**Hebrews 11:6**]. Therefore, we must accept who God is and what His words say. We must live in obedience to His will in order to please Him. If the individual has no faith, he or she will not hear from God. No one will be able to withstand against the wiles of the devil, outside of faith. For the person who has no faith, heaven will not be real because there is no hope of life after death. **Faith is the key to our salvation, and to our future with Christ.**

Dead faith means just what it is, <u>dead</u>. There is no conviction concerning the truths of God's words, and there is doubt when it comes to receiving His promises. Dead faith is inactive, and has no substance or evidence to show that the individual is trusting in God. That person will doubt the promises and rather, will act on his or her intellect and abilities. Those persons seek for logic and proof before they will accept what the word says.

Discussion

i. What do you understand by spiritual growth?

ii. What are the necessary foods do we need for spiritual growth?

iii. From the two passages in **John 15**, an **II Peter 1**, what do you understand by living a life, which will result in spiritual growth?

iv. How important is faith to the life of the believer and spiritual growth?

v. Is it possible that someone can be saved for many years, and still found himself or herself in spiritual infancy?

vi. What are some situations, which hinder growth?

vii. What does faith in God means?

viii. What is active or dead faith?

Summary

As children of God, we must grow in grace and in the knowledge of our Lord and Saviour Jesus Christ [**II Peter 3:18**]. When we are filled with spiritual knowledge, wisdom, and understanding: we have stability to walk worthy of the Lord to please Him, and not live according to world standards. We will be fruitful [**John 15:1-7**]. Everything we do will testify of our walk with the Lord Jesus Christ and our life will bear the fruit of the Spirit [**Galatians 5:22-23**].

As we grow in the Lord, we become strong in him, and are not easily led astray by contrary doctrines and beliefs. We will be settled in Him, firmly grounded as we increase in knowledge. When we study the word of God, we grow in grace; we grow in the Lord, and become wise.

Peter told us, **But grow in grace, and in the knowledge of our Lord and Saviour Jesus Christ** [**II Peter 3:18**].

Similar to our physical body, our souls need nourishment. What we put in them [body and soul] is what will make us develop healthily, and normally. If we do not eat proper spiritual foods in the right proportions that will nourish us, we become spiritually sick.

Next, in order to be spiritually strong, we need faith. We must have faith to please God; otherwise, He will not accept us unless we believe that He is real or that He answers prayers. Nevertheless, our faith must be with works. Otherwise, faith is dead.

Finally, we must be attached to the True Vine in order to grow in grace through faith. Growth takes place if we are fed on the word of God, and have a strong relationship with him.

Suggestions for further reading

a.   Romans 4

b.   Hebrews 11

c.   Matthew 17:14-21

d.   Luke 8:43-48

e.   Luke 18:1-8

f.   James 2:14-26

_____

_____

_____

_____

_____

_____

_____

Section 4

The Lord Jesus Christ

Jesus is the most unique person ever walked upon the earth. His interaction with, and care for people were far above the experience and reports of any one, no matter how famous that person might have been. With the Lord Jesus Christ, everything about Him is good. There is nothing in His character, which differs from Himself. His name is holy and has power. The blood, which was shed on mount Calvary, has virtue to cleanse, pardon, and deliver from sin. That same blood after all these thousands of years; still has power to heal and save. When the enemy attacks we use, claim, and apply the Blood of Jesus Christ against him; and he must flee. According to the word, **And they overcame him by the blood of the Lamb, and by the word of their testimony; and they loved not their lives unto the death** [**Revelations 12:11**]. The topics covered in this section are as follows:

a. Who is Jesus Christ?

b. Steps to Knowing the Lord Jesus Christ

c. The Redemptive Work of Jesus Christ

d. Jesus Reigns Supreme

_____
_____
_____
_____
_____
_____
_____
_____
_____
_____
_____
_____
_____

Who is Jesus Christ
Lesson 1

John 1:1-5, 14-18, 5:22-36-47, John 17:1-5, Philippians 2:5-16, Colossians 2

Introduction

Jesus is one of those persons whose story will never end. Many philosophers and great men came before and after Him, but most are forgotten with only a monument as evidence of their advent. Some died without a token of their past left behind. Yet Jesus the Son of God lives on, and will forever be in the hearts of mankind.

We cannot link Jesus Christ with any other person, spirit, or gods. He is **above all principalities and powers**. He is the **image of the invisible God, the firstborn of every creature... Colossians 1:15-29**. Jesus is highly exalted above everything and everyone [**Philippians 2:9**]. Jesus is before all things and all things consist of and through Him. The Bible teaches that Jesus Christ was before the foundation of the world [**Colossians 1:17**]. **John 17:5** is an endorsement of Jesus acknowledging His relationship with the Father; and affirming that He was before the beginning of time.

The responses to *"Who is Jesus Christ."*

1. He is our Redeemer: In the book of *Job*, we read his declaration stating: **For I know that my redeemer lives, and that he shall stand at the latter day upon the earth,** [**Job 19:25**]. He believed in Jesus Christ before His manifestation on earth.

2. He is our Strength: **David** made a plea to God, **Let the words of my mouth, and the meditation of my heart, be acceptable in thy sight, O Lord, my strength, and my redeemer**, [**Psalm 19:14**].

3. He is a Protector: The prophet **Isaiah**, shows how He calms, encourages, strengthens, and protects [**Isaiah 41:10**].

> **To redeem** means to exchange, buy back, transfer, release, liberate, deliver, or to set free. In other words, it means freedom for someone who otherwise, should have been charged, dead or held because of something the individual did.

4. Isaiah 41:14, Fear not, thou worm Jacob, and ye men of Israel, I will help thee, saith the Lord, and thy redeemer, the Holy One of Israel.

5. He is a Provider: Isaiah 41:17-20, When the poor and needy seek water, and there is none, and their tongue fails for thirst, I the Lord will hear them.

His Position with God, the Father

Jesus is the second Person in the Godhead, and in Him dwells all the fullness [substance] of the Godhead [Colossians 2:9, For in him dwells all the fullness of the Godhead bodily]. This means that by accepting Jesus Christ into our lives we are made complete in Him. [Colossians 2:10, And ye are complete in him, which is the head of all principality and power]. No one who ever lived, or is to come has this eminence with Almighty God. The Bible teaches that Jesus is the image of God, II Corinthians 4:4. Jesus Himself said, I am the way, the truth, and the life: no man comes unto the Father, but by me, [John 14:6].

At His baptism, the Father acknowledged Him by saying, This is my beloved Son, in whom I am well pleased, [Matthew 3:17]. Moreover, the angels of heaven worship Him stating, Thou art worthy, O Lord, to receive glory and honour and power: for thou has created al things, and for thy pleasure they are and were created, [Revelation 4:11].

He is the only one who lived as both God and man, all at the same time. The Father was so pleased that He glorified his name through Him when Jesus said, Father, glorify thy name. The response from the Father was, I have both glorified it, and will glorify it again [John 12:28].

Jesus is Highly Exalted

Philippians 2:9-11:

Wherefore God also hath highly exalted Him, and given him a name which is above every name; [9]

That at the name of Jesus every knee should bow, of things in heaven, and things in the earth, and things under the earth; [10]

And that every tongue should confess that Jesus Christ is Lord, to the glory of God the Father. [11]

> **Highly exalted:**
> This is an exaltation to the highest position. This is a level above all others. Jesus' obedience to the Father promoted Him to this position of glory, honour, and glorification.

_____

_____

_____

_____

_____

Attributes Pertaining to Jesus Christ

1. Jesus is the Saviour of the world. **For God so loved the world, that he gave his only begotten Son, that whosoever believes in him should not perish, but have everlasting life. For God sent not his Son into the world to condemn the world; but that the world through him might be saved. He that believes on him is not condemned: but he that believes not is condemned already because he hath not believed in the name of the only begotten Son of God [John 3:16-18].**

2. Jesus is the Son of God, which refers to His deity. **Matthew 3:17, And lo a voice from heaven, saying, This is my beloved Son, in whom I am well pleased.** He came to earth in human flesh to redeem us from our sins and to restore us back into fellowship with God.

3. Jesus is the Anointed One, **And Simon answered and said, Thou art the Christ, the Son of the living God, [Matthew 16:16].**

   Christ means Anointed

4. Jesus has a prominent place and relationship with the Father, even when He was on earth. **All things are delivered unto me of my Father: and no man knows the Son, but the Father; neither does any man know the Father, save the Son, and he to whomsoever the Son will reveal him, [Matthew 11:27].**

5. God sent Jesus Christ into the world to reconcile us back to Himself.
   And all things are of God, who hath reconciled us to himself by Jesus Christ, and hath given to us the ministry of reconciliation;
   To wit that God was in Christ, reconciling the world unto himself, not imputing their trespasses unto them; and hath committed unto us the word of reconciliation [II Corinthians 5:18-19].

6. Jesus is the Son of Man. **But that ye may know that the Son of man hath power upon earth to forgive sins... [Luke 5:24].**

7. Jesus is the Lamb of God. **The next day John sees Jesus coming unto him, and saith, Behold the Lamb of God, which takes away the sin of the world [John 1:29].**

8. Jesus, the Teacher. **And they were astonished at his doctrine: for he taught them as one that had authority, and not as the scribes [Mark 1:22].**

9. Jesus is the True Vine. **I am the true vine, and my Father is the husbandman [John 15:1].**

10. Jesus is God with us. **Behold a virgin shall conceive, and bear a son, and shall call his name Immanuel [Isaiah 7:14].**

11. <u>Jesus is the Greatest Leader</u>. **For unto us a child is born, unto us a son is given: and the government shall be upon his shoulder: and his name shall be called Wonderful, Counselor, The Mighty God, The everlasting Father, The Prince of Peace [Isaiah 9:6].**

12. <u>Jesus gave us life</u>. **I am come that they might have life, and that they might have it more abundantly [John 10:10b].**

    In this was manifested the love of God toward us, because that God sent his only begotten Son into the world, that we might live through him [I John 4:9].

13. <u>Jesus is the Propitiation for our sins</u>. **Herein is love, not that we loved God, but that he loved us, and sent his Son to be the propitiation for our sins [I John 4:10].**

14. <u>He is Mighty</u>: **For their redeemer is mighty, he shall plead their cause with thee, [Proverbs 23:11].**

    For the Lord will plead their cause, and spoil the soul of those that spoiled them, [Proverbs 22:23].

> **Propitiation:** *hilasmos*, Jesus is both the Sacrifice and the High Priest who approach God on our behalf to appease His wrath against us. Instead, we receive mercy and forgiveness.

How can we know the Lord Jesus?

1. We know Jesus from the **testimonies of witnesses** who walked with Him when He was on earth [I John 1:1-3].
2. **Having fellowship with Him [Romans 8:14, 1 John 1:5-7].**
3. **By believing that He is the Son of God, and accepting His word to be true.** Jesus was in Heaven with His Father before the world began, [**Colossians 1:17**].
4. We know Jesus by our **obedience [John 1:12].**
5. Through **faith** in believing that He came in flesh, [**John 1:1-14, Romans 10:9-10, I John 4:1-3**].
6. We must believe that **He came into the world to save all sinners [Romans 3:10-23].**

Why Jesus came to Earth

1. **To reconcile us back to God** so that we could be in fellowship with Him - **Romans 5:10-11. II Corinthians 5:18**. To reconcile means to restore relationship; to make things right; and to remove enmity. This could only be done through the <u>death</u>, <u>burial</u>, and <u>resurrection</u> of Jesus Christ. Sin separated us from God when Adam and Eve fell into disobedience. Their behaviour separated us from God, which brought us under His wrath. Jesus came to appease the Father so that His wrath would not come down upon us. Jesus forgives sins, and when He forgives our sins, God forgives us.

2. **To make us Children of God 1 John 3:1-2**. As children of God, we are transformed into His likeness when we receive Jesus in our lives. This cannot take place until we accept Him as God's Son, obey His word, and walk in His way. Now that we become Children of God we have access to the same privileges that God gives to His Son Jesus Christ because we have been adopted into the Family of God [**Romans 8:12-17**]. This simply means that we can approach God's presence in the Name of Jesus, and with His blood upon us. God will not accept any other Name. We must approach in prayer with reverence in the Name of Jesus.

3. **To give us Eternal Life - John 3:16**. In order to obtain this life, we must be born again. This means that we must believe on the Lord Jesus Christ from our hearts, and accept Him as our indwelling Lord and Saviour. We are baptized in water and the Holy Spirit seals us as God's property [**Ephesians 1:13**]. We also have access to receive the baptism in the Holy Spirit Who gives us spiritual gifts that help us in our walk with the Lord. We must believe that he came into the world to save us because we are all sinners - **Romans 3:10-23**

4. **Jesus Came to *Forgive us of our sins* - Matthew 9:4-6**

5.   **Jesus came to fulfill the law – Romans 8:3-4**

6.   **To make us Children of God – I John 3:1-2**

7.   **To bring us to Repentance – Matthew 9:13, John 1:12**

9.   **To forgive our sins – Matthew 9:4-6**

10.   **To be the Supreme Sacrifice for *sin* – Romans 3:25, 5:6-8**

Prophecies about the Lord Jesus Christ

    a.   **Isaiah 9:6-7, Deuteronomy 18:15, Acts 3:22-26,**

    b.   **Isaiah 53 – speaks of Jesus' atoning death on Calvary**

    c.   **Daniel 3:25 – He was the fourth man in the fire**

    d.   **Joshua 5:13-15 – Jesus appeared as Captain of the Lord's host**

Discussions

i. What do you know about Jesus Christ? Where do you place Him in your life?

ii. Do you believe that Jesus is indeed real and that He actually rose from the dead?

iii. If you believe Jesus is real, what makes you accept this claim?

iv. What can you tell someone from another religious order about the Jesus you know?

v. Do you think Jesus was harsh in saying that He would cut off anyone who does not bear fruit?

vi. What did the prophets say about Jesus? Do their prophecies make you believe on Him?

vii. Why did Jesus come to this world knowing He would have died such a cruel death?

viii. What are some attributes of Jesus Christ you notice are lacking in your life?

Who is Jesus Christ?

Lesson 2: Steps to Knowing the Lord Jesus

John 3, I John 2:7-14, 4:7-21

Introduction

There are many who will say that all religions lead to a saving faith in the Lord Jesus Christ. Maybe this is arguable depending on what an individual believes. However, those who are of the Christian faith know that the only way we can know Him is by accepting Him through the new birth. When Nicodemus went to Jesus to find out about His teachings and how he could obtain eternal life, Jesus told him plainly **Verily, verily, I say unto thee, Except a man be born again, he cannot see the kingdom of God, [John 3:3]**. Evidently, Nicodemus was puzzled and reasoned, **How can a man be born when he is old: can he enter the second time into his mother's womb, and be born? [John 3:4]**. No one can blame Nicodemus for his naïveté and lack of understanding about spiritual matters. It was a reasonable question, because what Jesus told him surely did not sound logical. Yet, Jesus was right on target. The New Birth is about spiritual things and not earthly.

The New Birth

It is clearly laid out in **John 3**, that for anyone to come to Jesus Christ, that person must experience the New Birth. Jesus said, **Verily, verily, I say unto thee, Except a man be born of water and of the Spirit, he cannot enter into the kingdom of God, [John 3:5ff]**. Moreover, Jesus is the entrance, [door] to *Salvation* **John 10:9, I am the door: by me if any man enter in, he shall be saved, and shall go in and out, and find pasture.**

Jesus is the path to *knowing* God – **John 14:6, Jesus said; I am the way, the truth, and the life: no man comes unto the Father, but by me.**

The Born Again person believes that Jesus came into the flesh. **I John 4:2-3, Hereby know ye the Spirit of God: Every spirit that confesses that Jesus Christ is come in the flesh is of God:**

And every spirit that confesses not that Jesus Christ is come in the flesh is not of God: and this is that (*spirit*) of antichrist, whereof ye have heard that it should come; and even now already is it in the world.

Repentance: A Changed Life

When we speak of the New Birth, what do we really mean? What does it signifies in the life of the individual? What is the New Birth?

In answer to all those questions, we could agree that the New Birth is a life, which is spiritual and completely different from what we have ever known. It means a spiritual encounter with the Lord Jesus Christ through the Holy Spirit. He is the one who brings conviction to the sinner making him or her repent, and turn towards a new life in, and with Christ.

The New Birth leads to a changed life whereby the individual allows the Holy Spirit to carry out the process of sanctification to separate him or her from worldliness. This is a daily activity **[Luke 9:23]**.

Evidently, there must be qualitative change beginning with the acknowledgement of sin, which leads to repentance; baptism in water; and baptism in the Holy Spirit who will conduct the ongoing process of sanctification as the individual yields to Him. The world must see the change because Christianity is not a private affair [**Matthew 5:13-16**].

In addition, the new believer must belong to a local church. It is his or her responsibility to stay close to the Lord through church attendance, Bible reading, prayer, and fasting. Indeed, it is a changed life from the usual.

Having a Personal Relationship with Jesus

1. Willingness to suffer for Him – **Philippians 3:10; Luke 9:23, I Peter 4**
2. Forgiveness of Sin – **Romans 3:24-26, John 3:16-17, 6:47-59**
3. **Prayer – consistent – Colossians 4:2, I Thessalonians 5:17**
4. **Testimonies** of *healing, deliverances, provisions, and protection*

Maintaining *active* Relationship with Jesus Christ

1. **Connection** - in your daily life, constant in prayer - *reading* and *applying* the word, *obedience* – **John 15**
2. **Prune/Purged/Sufferings - John 15:2**
3. **Disobedience/Separation/Spiritual Death - John 15:6**
4. **Obedience which leads to a Fruitful Life – John 15: 4-7, Galatians 5:22-23**
5. **Special Favour** – John **15:7, 10, 23**

Separation from the World

According to **Colossians 3:1, If ye then be risen with Christ, seek those things which are above, where Christ sits on the right hand of God.** Paul encouraged us that as believers, we must seek the things, which bring honour and glory to God rather than for those we indulged in before salvation, which brought destruction and separation from God, and death.

When we come to know Christ, we are become new creatures [*spiritual* **II Peter 1:4**]. We receive a new nature depicting the divine nature of God. This can only be accomplished through the blood of Jesus Christ. Living for Jesus gives us access to His eternal glory when we will live with Him forever. We must show ourselves to be Christ-like in our behaviour and character. We cannot be like those who do not know Him.

_____

_____

_____

_____

_____

_____

_____

_____

_____

_____

_____

_____

_____

_____

_____

_____

_____

_____

_____

_____

_____

_____

_____

_____

_____

_____

_____

_____

The Redemptive Work of Jesus

Psalm 49:6-9, Ephesians 1:3-14, 2:11-22

Introduction

Psalm 49:6-9

They that trust in their wealth, and boast themselves in the multitude of their riches; [6]

None of them can by any means redeem his brother, nor give to God a ransom for him: [7]

(For the redemption of their souls is precious, and it ceases forever:) [8]

That he should still live forever, and not see corruption. [9]

Ephesians 1:3-7, 13-14

Blessed be the God and Father of Jesus Christ, who hath blessed us with all spiritual blessings in heavenly (*places*) in Christ: [3]

According as he hath chosen us in him before the foundation of the world, that we should be holy and without blame before him in love: [4]

Having predestined us unto the adoption of children by Jesus Christ to himself, according to the good pleasure of his will, [5]

To the praise of the glory of his grace, wherein he hath made us accepted in the beloved. [6]

In whom we have redemption through his blood, the forgiveness of sins, according to the riches of his grace; [7]

In whom ye also (*trusted*), after that ye heard the word of truth, the gospel of your salvation: in whom also after that ye believed, ye were sealed with that Holy Spirit of promise, [13]

Which is the earnest of our inheritance until the redemption of the purchased possession, unto the praise of his glory. [14]

_____
_____
_____
_____

Our Redemption

The Bible tells us that riches cannot purchase our salvation. It cannot redeem us or give us a good conscience. Riches are of no value when it comes to the redemption of our souls [**Psalm 49:6-9**]. The price on our heads was great, demanding a special kind of currency to free us from the bondage of sin's grasp.

Furthermore, we were born as sinners with the sin DNA in us [**Psalm 51:5**]. There was nothing we could have done, to purchase our redemption. **The blood of animals could not do it.** The blood of animals could only do a partial work, which had to be repeated every year. **But in those (***sacrifices there***) is a remembrance again (***made***) of sins every year**, [Hebrews 10:3].

Neither by the blood of goats and calves, but by his own blood he entered in once into the holy place, having obtained eternal redemption (*for us***), [Hebrews 9:12].**

For it was not possible that the blood of bulls and of goats should take away sins, [Hebrew 10:4].

The Blood of Jesus Christ

Before Jesus made His appearance, the priests had to offer sacrifices for sins every year. It was a repetitious act requiring the killing of animals. Each family had to offer up for the household, and the priest had to offer up for himself and his house. If he were unworthy, he would die behind the vail.

According to the word, **And almost all things are by the law purged with blood; and without shedding of blood is no remission [Hebrews 9:22]**. Nevertheless, it took a special kind of blood. It must be pure, sinless, untainted by Adam's sin. Jesus gave us salvation who, **by his own blood he entered in once into the holy place, having obtained eternal redemption for us**, [Hebrews 9:12b].

Paul warned pastors concerning the people of God and the blood of Jesus Christ, **Take heed therefore unto yourselves, and to all the flock, over the which the Holy Ghost hath made you overseers, to feed the church of God, which he hath purchased with his own blood, [Acts 20:28].**

Jesus's death, burial, and resurrection gave us ...**redemption through his blood, the forgiveness of sins, according to the riches of his grace, [Ephesians 1:7].**

Clearly, the foundation of our salvation is enveloped in the grace, mercy, and love of God who sent His only Son Jesus Christ to die for our sins. It is the redeeming blood of Jesus, which gives us freedom from the penalty of sin. Furthermore, Jesus' death gives us wisdom, which is practical knowledge and spiritual principles for application of His word. Through the Holy Spirit, we obtain this knowledge by revelation, with clear perception and understanding [**Ephesians 1:17**].

There is no illusion when it comes to the understanding of God's word. Once we have accepted the Lord Jesus Christ in our lives, we are no longer living in darkness, but in clear view of spiritual wisdom and knowledge.

Jesus is the **Head of the Body of Believers** here on earth [**I Corinthians 11:3, Ephesians 1:22**], who represent the church. Each member is a saint and attached to Jesus Christ [**John 15:1**] by His blood. This relationship is obtained by **grace** [**Ephesians 2:8**], **through faith**, and the power of the Holy Spirit. No one can minister effectively without the power of the Holy Spirit, and grace operates through faith by the power of the Spirit.

Reconciliation with God, Ephesians 2:11-22

But now in Christ Jesus ye who sometimes were far of are made nigh by the blood of Christ. [13]

For he is our peace, who hath made both one, and hath broken down the middle wall of partition (*between us*); [14]

And that he might reconcile both unto God in one body by the cross, having slain the enmity thereby: [16]

And came and preached peace to you which were afar off, and to them that were nigh. [17]

Jesus was the only One who could re-connect us to God. This reconciliation brought peace with man and God [**Colossians 1:20-22**]. We must remain in fellowship with Jesus Christ to obtain the fullness of His presence in our lives [**Colossians 1:23, John 15:1-7**]. When we receive Jesus Christ in our lives, we must make every effort to live for Him in obedience and humility.

_____
_____
_____
_____
_____
_____
_____
_____
_____
_____
_____
_____
_____
_____
_____
_____
_____
_____
_____
_____

Section 5

Renounce Worldliness

Jesus said, **No man can serve two masters: for either he will hate the one, and love the other: or else he will hold to the one, and despise the other. Ye cannot serve God and mammon [Matthew 6:24, Luke 16:13].** Anyone who tries to serve God while still living for the devil, is a hypocrite. The text fully bears this out that no one can serve two masters. Apparently, those who are in this category do not think they can live for God without still holding on to the attachments of the world. Serving the Lord Jesus Christ is a serious step of faith and cannot be tampered with by trying to adjust to worldliness at the same time. The individual **must have a made up mind** to serve the Lord in spirit and in truth. That individual **must renounce the world** and its attractions for total devotion and obedience to the Lord.

Put *off* the Old Man

    a.   Introduction

    b.   Vanity of the Mind

    c.   Darkened Understanding

    d.   Alienation from God

    e.   Hearts of Stone

    f.   Insensitivity

Put *on* the New Man

    a.   Renewed Mind

    b.   Holiness

    c.   Honesty

    d.   Self-control

    e.   Usefulness

    f.   Conduct

Renounce Worldliness
Lesson 1: The Old Man of Sin
Ephesians 4:17-23, Colossians 3: 5-11

Introduction

There are people who claim they have a relationship with Jesus Christ, yet their behaviour and lifestyle tell a different tale. No one can serve two masters simultaneously: he must devote himself to one or the other. Despite this fact, the argument is that it does not take all the seriousness and holiness, which the word declares we should portray before the world **[I Peter 1:13-16]**. No one can live for Christ and the world at the same time. It would be impossible to even attempt this since both require specific attention and loyalty. When God speaks of holiness, He means being set apart for His service. We cannot serve Him and the devil at the same time. There must be a determined choice for one or the other.

Colossians 3:5-11

Mortify therefore your members which are upon the earth; fornication, uncleanness, inordinate affection, evil concupiscence, and covetousness, which is idolatry: [5]

For which things' sake the wrath of God comes on the children of disobedience: [6]

In the which ye also walked some time, when ye lived in them. [7]

But now ye also put off all these; anger, wrath, malice, blasphemy, filthy communication out of your mouth. [8]

Lie not one to another, seeing that ye have put off the old man with his deeds; [9]

And have put on the new man, which is renewed in knowledge after the image of him that created him: [10]

Where there is neither Greek nor Jew, circumcision nor uncircumcision, Barbarian, Scythia, bond nor free: but Christ is all, and in all. [11]

Fornication: *porneia*, pornography, illicit sexual activities, prostitution, incest, adultery, homosexuality, and habitual immorality. This includes both physical and spiritual immorality, which leads to idolatry.

Uncleanness: *akatharsía*, sexual impurity, sinfulness, immorality, lewdness, adulteration. Moral uncleanness, either with the self or others.

Evil Concupiscence: *epithumía*, lusts. A strong desire and intense craving for something forbidden. Striving for things, persons, or experiences contrary to the will of God. A diseased condition of the soul.

Wrath: *thumus*, inflammatory rage, impulsive outbursts of hot anger with the purpose for revenge.

Blasphemy: *blasphēmía*, abuse against someone, slander. Wounding someone's reputation.

Holiness [I Peter 1:13-16]

In the passage above, Paul lists the various things that were enmity between us, and God. He encouraged and instructed us to leave those things behind and seek after spiritual things. He showed that we cannot have one foot in the world and the other in the church. It will not work. We must be consistent with our living showing evidence of integrity and faithfulness.

The call of God is holiness because He is holy. We must acknowledge our weaknesses and recognize that we cannot please God in ourselves. We need the Holy Spirit's presence and power to live faithful upright lives.

Our flesh must be crucified so that we can walk in the Spirit to please a holy God [**Galatians 5:16, 24**]. The things of this world must not have pre-eminence in our lives, thus pushing away the Holy Spirit. No one can serve God truthfully with unclean vessels [**I Corinthians 6:20**].

Our bodies do not belong to us; they belong to Christ. We must change from who we were, the persons we were, and from the things we did before knowing Jesus Christ. Those things were sinful and brought separation between us, and God.

Ephesians 4:17-23

This I say therefore, and testify in the Lord, that ye henceforth walk not as other Gentiles walk, in the vanity of their mind, [17]

Vanity: *mátaiotes*, vain, nothingness, worthlessness.

Having the understanding darkened, being alienated from the life of God through the ignorance that is in them, because of the blindness of their heart: [18]

Who being past feeling have given themselves over unto lasciviousness, to work all uncleanness with greediness. [19]

But ye have not so learned Christ. [20]

If so be that ye have heard him, and have been taught by him, as the truth is in Jesus. [21]

That ye put off concerning the former conversation the old man, which is corrupt according to the deceitful lusts. [22]

And be renewed in the spirit of your mind; [23]

People, who fall into those categories or any of the traits, characteristically demonstrate a love for the world by accepting what it has to offer. They indulge in its dainties, and do not separate themselves as the Scriptures admonished Christians to do.

All Christians should make every effort to give up the things of the world and surrender to the will of God. We must forsake behaviours, which are destructive by rejecting the attractions they offer. Worldliness is always present in the lives of weak Christians where there is lack of substance, unholy behaviours, insecurities, insincerity, hollowness, pride, foolishness, and a host of other descriptive evidences.

The Scripture identifies features of worldliness seen in the Christian church today. This is nothing new, but it has become more evident and ingrained among the people of God or those who are *professors of Christianity*. The features include the following: <u>vanity of the mind</u>, <u>darkened understanding</u>, <u>alienation from God</u>, <u>hardness of the heart</u>, and <u>insensitivity</u>.

_____
_____
_____
_____
_____
_____
_____
_____
_____
_____
_____
_____
_____
_____
_____
_____
_____

Lesson 2: Put off the Old Man

Ecclesiastes 2:1-17, Ephesians 4:17-23, Colossians 3:5-11, I Timothy 6:6-11

Vanity of the Mind

In **Ecclesiastes 1:1**, Solomon gave a concise description about vanity, saying **Vanity of vanities, saith the Preacher, vanity of vanities; all is vanity.** Who would have expected such speech from a man whom God blessed with <u>wisdom</u> and <u>riches</u>? [**See II Chronicles 1**]. To think that at the end of his life all he could see was the *emptiness* and *futility* of his accomplishments. Apparently, he was disappointed with what he did with the blessings of God.

Seemingly, Solomon was assessing the value of his life and its attractions; he concluded that he was unhappy with it. He said, **Therefore I hated life; because the work that is wrought under the sun is grievous unto me: for all is vanity and vexation of spirit,** [Ecclesiastes 2:4-17].

This sounds incredible coming from someone such as Solomon. He noted how wearisome life can be. He stated, **All things are full of labour; man cannot utter it: the eye is not satisfied with seeing, nor the ear filled with hearing,** [Ecclesiastes 1:8]. This speaks of dissatisfaction with possessions. He showed that **the more we accumulate, the more we go after because we are not satisfied with what we already have.**

Pleasure: Ecclesiastes 2:1-3

I said in mine heart, Go to now, I will prove thee with mirth, therefore enjoy pleasure; and, behold, this also is vanity. [1]
I said of laughter, It is mad: and of mirth, What does it? [2]
I sought in mine heart to give myself unto wine, yet acquainting mine heart with wisdom; and to lay hold on folly, till I might see what was that good for the sons of men, which they should do under the heaven all the days of their life. [3]
From the text above one could see that Solomon's next observation concerning vanity relates to going after <u>pleasure</u>. While recreation is good for us, yet we should not make this our main priority for happiness and fulfillment. Pleasure must be a source of enjoyment to relieve us from emotional pressures: rather than something we go after at the expense of our <u>peace</u>, <u>contentment</u> and even our <u>soul</u>.

We see at the end of Solomon's life how unhappy he was. There must be a good reason for placing this portion of Scripture in the word of God. Truly, it is for our learning, and for us to pay heed.

Solomon did not only go after pleasure for the sake of being happy; but he wanted to find out if it was worthwhile. One might even say that he did a research on the subject [**I sought in mine heart to give myself unto wine, yet acquainting mine heart with wisdom, Ecclesiastes 2:3**].

This does not sound like passion, but real interest because he wanted to know if pleasure was a good thing. It could be that the result of his quest must have been negative considering his speech towards the end of his life.

Emptiness of the Mind

This I say therefore, and testify in the Lord, that ye henceforth walk not as other Gentiles walk, in the vanity of their mind, [Ephesians 4:17]

Vanity of the mind refers to thinking loosely without sense. **The Lord knows the thoughts of man, that they are vanity [Psalms 94:11]**. It is evidence of an unprincipled life without discipline or morals. There is emptiness and aimlessness, which does not lead to any identifiable end. It reveals a useless lifestyle without meaning or substance.

The speech, which comes from such persons, is empty and filled with humanistic or selfish philosophies. They talk about Christianity, but do not have any defined understanding or knowledge to interpret the doctrine of Jesus Christ in order to help themselves or others.

The mind is vain and empty and without object or purpose. There is no eternal future for vain individuals. The reason is that they live for themselves and for the present. The vain mind is destitute of spiritual and moral wisdom. They are stubborn, tenacious, irrational, and foolish concerning their own beliefs. The blindness of their eyes and, hardness of their hearts separate them from truth and reality.

Lack of Purpose

The vain mind has no purpose. The life that lacks purpose or plan will lead to futility. Someone who believes in God and seeks to please Him will have a determined mind to do the things, which please Him. The reason is that the person has a precise goal to spend eternity with the Lord. Life is spent with that expectation of a future, which will surpass anything mankind has ever known.

In the natural sense, a life without purpose is aimless without desire for better or self-improvement. There is no meaning or devotion for anything that is worthwhile and no future or aspiration. Instead, that person lives only for the day and grasps at straw. He or she sows to the wind with no hope of ever achieving anything substantial [**Hosea 8:7**].

Darkened Understanding

Having the understanding darkened, [**Ephesians 4:18a**] refers to the intellect, seared by worldly standards and incorrect interpretation of spiritual principles [**I Timothy 4:2**]. That person is not able to see clearly in the wisdom of God's word. He or she has a **form of godliness, but denying the power thereof: from such turn away,** [**II Timothy 3:5**].

The darkened understanding leads to lack of wisdom because the person is ever learning, but never coming to or understanding the word [**II Timothy 3:7**]. People in this category are easily led into falsehood and misinterpretation of God's word. They are unstable and moves with every wind of doctrine [**Ephesians 4:14**].

The person whose understanding is in obscurity, no longer knows truth from fiction [**I Timothy 4:1**]. Since the person does not see the need for knowing God, the very truth of God's word remains hidden even though the individual might be a church-goer. There is doubt and confusion, faithlessness, unbelief, with the mind blocked from learning or understanding the truth of the doctrine of Christ.

Wisdom is to make us wise, but if we do not study God's word, and listen for the Holy Spirit's guidance, we will be led astray [**II Timothy 2:15**].

Too many believers do not attend Bible Study – Sunday morning or in the week. Yet, many desire to teach others about what they know, which is often distorted and mixed with worldly philosophies.

If the understanding is darkened, blurred by worldliness, humanism, and selfish attitudes, then that individual will live in error.

There will be poor judgment concerning the things of God. Some believers are living in sin with the hope of spending eternity with Jesus, because, according to the common man, he is only human.

With a darkened understanding, it is difficult to determine truth in order to accept God's word. That heart is opened to all kinds of fallacies and doctrines, which are alien to the word of God.

Note that our minds are constantly engaged in activity all day long. We think about all manner of things – the good, the bad, and the indifferent.

Sometimes we do discriminate, but there are occasions when we tarry too long with a thought, which often becomes an obsession. It is being preoccupied about something we think we should have, which makes us dissatisfied with life.

Nevertheless, if we are not careful, whatever comes to our minds we will concentrate on that image? Therefore, we must be vigilant concerning the thoughts, which come to our mind. Those thoughts must be in agreement with **Philippians 4:8**. If we adhere to this advice, we will never go wrong.

Food for Thought

i.   Let us consider the life of Solomon and reassess our *purpose* and *aim* in life.

ii.   Ask yourself if you are happy or if what you possess is a burden because you are dissatisfied with your lot.

iii.   Each individual must define what he or she understands happiness to mean.

iv.   What will you do with the opportunities and accomplishments in your life?

v.   Are you content with what you have? [**See I Timothy 6:6-11**].

_____

_____

_____

_____

_____

_____

_____

_____

_____

_____

_____

_____

_____

_____

_____

_____

_____

_____

_____

_____

_____

_____

_____

_____

Lesson 3: Alienation from God

Ephesians 4:18b

Introduction

To be alienated means <u>estrangement</u>, <u>isolation</u>, <u>indifference</u>, and <u>separation</u>. The person who has alienated himself from God will be hostile and unfriendly toward those who purpose to live closely to Him. The true believer is like an impediment to the worldly person/hypocrite. The alienated individual has a broken relationship with God. He has transferred allegiance and committed spiritual adultery. That person has become a stranger to God's grace.

Alienation is abandonment and separation from what is real to that, which is false. That person, who has been cleansed and purged from dead works, returns to the [**weak and beggarly elements, Galatians 4:9**]. They return similar to **the dog to its vomit, and the sow to its wallow in the mud** [II Peter 2:21-22].

Separation leads to division, disunity, disconnection and severance. When a member of the body of Jesus Christ alienates himself or herself from Him and the true doctrine, that person may still attend some kind of worship service, but the heart is not with God.

According to **Isaiah 29:13, Forasmuch as this people draw near me with their mouth, and with their lips do honour me, but have removed their heart far from me, and their fear toward me is taught by the precept of men.**

Ignorance

The person who separates himself from God will go after strange gods, doctrines, values, and beliefs [**I Timothy 4:1**]. That person does not have the understanding of God's word and will accept faulty interpretation of the word from those who are disobedient and estranged from the true principles of the doctrine of Christ.

> **Ignorance:** *agnola,* lack of knowledge, carelessness, thoughtlessness.

Ignorance of God's word will lead into the bosom of hell. If people do not know God, they live a life of misconduct, irritability, rashness, angry outbursts, and all kinds of unsociable behaviours.

The Bible teaches, **My people are destroyed for lack of knowledge: because thou has rejected knowledge, I will also reject thee, that thou shalt be no priest to me: seeing thou has forgotten the law of thy God, I will also forget thy children**, [Hosea 4:6].

Our minds are constantly working and we seek for meaning and understanding about worldviews and events. All those answers are in the word of God. However, if someone rejects knowledge, that person will remain in ignorance, which will keep him or her from the presence of God.

Ignorance is the result of lack of cognition concerning truth, wisdom, and understanding, willful sinning, carelessness and lack of self-control. Those persons are thoughtless and act without conscience or consideration for consequences. They are presumptuous, unholy, immoral, and ungodly.

_____
_____
_____
_____
_____
_____
_____
_____
_____
_____
_____
_____
_____
_____
_____
_____
_____
_____
_____
_____

Lesson 4: Heart of Stone – *hardened, blind*

Having the understanding darkened, being alienated from the life of God through the ignorance that is in them, because of the blindness of their heart: [Ephesians 4:18

> **Blindness** means hardness of the heart. Spiritual blindness.

The hardened heart will result in disobedience. People stumble at the word because their spiritual eyes have become darkened. **Jeremiah 17:9-10**, speaks of the callousness of a cold, insensitive, hard heart. Jesus further showed that out a hardened heart proceeds all manner of evil **[Matthew 15:19]**.

A hardened heart is unfeeling. There is self-interest and self-centeredness with no regard for anyone else but the needs and desires of the self. Those persons treat others with callousness, cruelty, and pitilessness. They are uncaring and unfeeling because the Holy Spirit no longer rules in the life [*See* **II Timothy 3:2-7**].

Lasciviousness

Who being past feeling have given themselves over unto lasciviousness, to work all uncleanness with greediness, [Ephesians 4:19].
Having their conscience seared with a hot iron, [I Timothy 4:2].

> **Lasciviousness**
> Means licentiousness. Wickedness, lusts, shameless, indecencies, unrestrained depravity. Sinning openly.

These are ungodly people, who no longer feel sorrow for sin, but rather enjoy its charms as they delve into its dainties. The person living in lasciviousness is without concern for misconduct because he or she no longer feels sorrow for sin. They will ignore warnings and consider a rebuke as judging.

Uncleanness

This behaviour refers to all manner of spiritual, moral, and physical behaviour. There is spiritual impurity as the mind becomes polluted with all manner of spiritual sins of the thoughts, habits, and attitudes.

Uncleanness affects the mind and body and evidenced in the behaviour and conversation. Those persons will be proponents of ungodliness, and will break marital vows. They live for the present, and have no thought for the coming of the Lord. This does not say they will not attend church.

Some are even leaders in the church, whose lives are contrary in relation to morality and spirituality. Even in their marriage, they will introduce immoral acts and devices to satisfy their lascivious desires. They live according to world standards, and do not consider uncleanness a problem. Instead, it becomes a way of life.

Uncleanness leads to unnatural affections [**Romans 1:28-32**], separating them from the presence of God. Although they may be regular church-goers, attendance does not necessarily mean godliness. It can be completely contrary with God's desires for holiness and upright living. Unnatural affections lead to abomination, and all manner of physical, moral, and spiritual evils.

Greediness

There are people who go out of their way to gain materialistic things. Although in some cases, they have more than enough. Seemingly, they are not satisfied, and will go after more even if it cost them the family, health, or their soul. Greed means an insatiable appetite for more and more, until there is need for a bigger barn to put all the accumulated things. There is over-indulgence of anything the heart desires.

Insensitivity

The behaviour of insensitivity summarizes the entire passage of **Ephesians 4:17-23** because the insensitive Christian has no feelings concerning sin and its consequences. The reason is that the spirit of insensitivity gives a false sense of security and lends itself to some kind of happiness and peaceful existence. Yet, it is temporary and brings shame and distress. The spirit of insensitivity is worldly and leads only to destruction and separation from God.

An insensitive person is unforgiving and selfish with no care for truth, holiness, morality, or others. Therefore, even when that person lives in lasciviousness, which is immorality, and unbridled feelings of lusts, it makes no difference. The reason is that the person sins openly with arrogance and delights in sin without remorse. The behaviour is one of depravity, and shamelessness without restraint.

_____
_____
_____
_____
_____
_____
_____
_____
_____
_____
_____

Discussion

i. How would you assess Solomon's life and the climax to his experience?

ii. Why do you think Solomon came to the conclusion that life is "vanity."

iii. What does wealth and happiness have to do with contentment?

iv. There are "Christians" who will tell you that their life is theirs' to live any way they desire. What is your response to this ideology?

v. Do you think that by reprimanding someone about sin, it is judging that person?

vi. Should pastors discipline wrong-doers in the church?

vii. Should pastors preach against sin?

viii. How should pastors deal with worldliness in the church?

Lesson 5: Put on the *New* Man

Colossians 3:10-17

Introduction

Colossians 3:10-17

And put on the new (*man*), which is renewed in knowledge after the image of him that created him: [10]

Put on therefore, as the elect of God, holy and beloved, bowels of mercies, kindness, humbleness of mind, meekness, longsuffering; [12]

Forbearing one another, and forgiving one another, if any man have a quarrel against any: even as Christ forgave you, so also (*do ye*). [13]

And above all these things (*put on*) charity, which is the bond of perfectness. [14]

And let the peace of God rule in your hearts, to the which also ye are called in one body; and be ye thankful. [15]

Let the word of Christ dwell in you richly in all wisdom; teaching and admonishing one another in psalms and hymns, and spiritual songs, singing with grace in your hearts to the Lord. [16]

And whatsoever ye do in word or deed, (*do*) all in the name of the Lord Jesus, giving thanks to God and the Father by Him. [17]

The operative themes in the text above are *change*, *patience*, *humility*, *forgiveness*, *love*, *peace*, *unity*, and *knowledge* of the word to encourage one another. It summarizes the manner in which Christians ought to live; the kinds of character traits we must possess, and the need to forgive and live holy.

We cannot subject ourselves to carnal weaknesses and desires as do worldly people.

Our lives must show that we have been changed, and that Christ is living in and through us. We are no longer our own, but we belong to the Lord Jesus Christ; and sin must not have dominion over our lives [Romans 6:12].

Five important points which refer to our *relationship* and *obedience* to God in **Colossians 3:12-17** indicate traits for bearing fruits of the Spirit [**Galatians 5:22-23**], and include a renewed mind, holiness, longsuffering, love towards one another, and giving praises to God.

A Renewed Mind

And be renewed in the spirit of your mind, [Ephesians 4:23]. To be renewed in the mind means making a complete change from what used to be, to what ought to be. **II Corinthians 5:17, Therefore if any man be in Christ, he is a new creature: old things are passed away; behold, all things are become new**. This refers to a complete radical qualitative change, which can be seen. It takes the work of the Holy Spirit and a truly repentant heart for the mind to be renewed. There should be a fresh identifiable start, even though it will take time; there must be an effort made for change. In such a life, the Holy Spirit is in control and directs the path of the individual [**Proverbs 3:5-6**]. All personal desires and ambitions are submitted to the Lord for His direction. The **renewed mind** refers to renovation, restoration, transformation, and a qualitative change of heart and life [**Romans 12:2**].

Holiness [*hagiosune*]

I Thessalonians 3:13, To the end he may stablish your hearts unblameable in holiness before God, even our Father, at the coming of our Lord Jesus Christ with all his saints.

Holiness means being set apart for God's purpose. It means our very conduct and interaction with others will portray a life, which is dedicated to the Lord.

Living a life of holiness is the principle, which separates the Christian from the world and its uncleanness. It is a consecrated life both body and soul, for the service and purpose of pleasing God. This life finds fulfillment in purity and not moral living. It is a changed life completely different from what used to be.

Holiness for the believer means character change with the determination to seek righteousness and purity at all cost. It is a life that is renewed according to **Ephesians 4:23**, which states, **And be renewed in the spirit of your mind**. [**See also Romans 12:2**].

To practice holiness means we must identify with the Lord Jesus through His character, and holiness. The world must see change in us. There should be no doubt in the minds of people identifying us with Christ in whom we believe and whom we serve, love, and trust. It must be noted that holiness is depicted in *family life* [**Colossians 3:18-21, see also Ephesians 6:1-4**]; and *on the job* [**Colossians 3:22-25, see also Ephesians 6:5-9**].

_____

_____

_____

i.   <u>Family Life and Holiness</u> Colossians 3:18-21

    Wives, submit yourselves unto your own husbands, as it is fit in the Lord. [18]

    Husbands, love your wives, and be not bitter against them. [19]

    Children, obey your parents in all things: for this is well pleasing unto the Lord. [20]

    Fathers, provoke not your children to anger, lest they be discouraged. [21]

ii. <u>Holiness on the Job</u> Colossians 3:22-25; 4:1

    Servants, obey in all things your masters according to the flesh; not with eye service, as men pleasers; but in singleness of heart, fearing God. [22]

    Masters, give unto your servants that which is just and equal; knowing that ye also have a Master in heaven [Colossians 4:1].

Longsuffering, <u>Patience</u> [*hupomonē*]

It is difficult to find people who are willing to wait on God because of the microwave age in which we live. Patience means *forbearance*, *humility*, *kindness*, *mercy*, *meekness*, and being able to *forgive* others from the heart [**Colossians 3:12**]. The patient person reflects one who has a changed life, renewed by the Blood of Jesus Christ. It shows a life in which, the Holy Spirit is in residence in the heart.

i.   **Forbearance** means having self-control, and restraint even when you have the right to speak up, yet you will hold your peace and wait for the right place and time. According to the word, **Stand in awe and sin not: commune with your own heart upon your bed, and be still**, [**Psalm 4:4**]. Think before you speak [**James 1:19**].

ii. **Practice self-control** [**Galatians 5:22-23**], and do not make opportunity for the devil to use you to carry out his plans. He is always searching for willing preys to be his next meal.

    Be sober, be vigilant; because your adversary the devil, as a roaring lion, walks about, seeking whom he may devour, [I Peter 5:8].

    Whom resist steadfast in the faith, knowing that the same afflictions are accomplished in your brethren that are in the world, [I Peter 5:9].

iii. **Humility**, while many consider humility to be weakness, this if far from the truth. The spirit of humility shows inner fortitude and is akin to meekness. The humble person has a place in the presence of God.

_____

_____

_____

_____

_____

iv.   **Kindness**: the kind person shows compassion and gentleness. There is genuine sympathy for others who are less fortunate economically, intellectually, physically, and spiritually.

v.   **Mercy**, the merciful is generous and patient, understanding, thoughtful, and gentle.

vi.   **Meekness** is modesty and submissiveness. It means giving way to others more often than holding on to rights. The meek person is disciplined, quiet, and humble.

vii.   **Forgive**, to forgive does not mean over-looking wrongs. Instead, it means releasing someone of a grudge from a hurt. Sometimes others offend us by a thoughtless word or deed, which hurt our feelings. Nevertheless, God expects us to forgive the individual. This does not mean you cannot discuss the matter with the offender, but you use kindness, mercy, humility, and patience when doing so. To forgive is extending love and mercy. Avoid being retaliative to prove a point or to win a dispute. Learn to forgive so that God's grace can work in your heart. Submit to God's will for confidence to overcome the enemy [**James 4:7**].

Love towards one another

I Corinthians 13:4-8, gives us a summation of sincere unconditional love. God demonstrated this type of love to Adam's fallen race.

1.   There must be no pretense or counterfeit whether in word or deed;

2.   Genuine love expressed with loyalty, warmth, care, empathy, with concern for the feelings of others;

3.   Love must be expressed in different ways such as patience, empathy, and kindness;

4.   Love not because of your personal desires; but for the desire of others.

Gratefulness to God

Praise should come naturally to the lips of the Christian. How often we call upon God when we are in trouble, but forget to thank and praise Him for His goodness. In **Psalm 50:14-15**, God encourages us to praise Him who is the Most High. God said, **Whoso offers praise glorifies me: and to him that orders his conversation aright will I show the salvation of God**, [Psalm 50:23[.

Additionally, if we desire God's favour, we are urged to give Him praise, [**Psalm 67:5-7**].

Let the people praise thee, O God; let all the people praise thee. [5

Then shall the earth yield her increase; and God, even our own God, shall bless us. [6]

God shall bless us; and all the ends of the earth shall fear him. [7]

I believe that **Psalm 33:1** sums it up with, **Rejoice in the Lord, O ye righteous: for praise is comely for the upright.**

Suggestions for further Reading

a. Psalm 107

b. Psalm 136

c. Psalm 150

d. I Corinthians 13:4-8

e. Galatians 5:22-23

f. Titus 3:5

Discussion

i. What does it mean by putting off the old man and putting on the new?

ii. What changes should be evident in the life of the believer who has renounced the world?

iii. How would you witness to someone who came to you from another religious faith?

iv. What changes have come into your life since you accepted the Lord Jesus Christ?

v. Do you believe the Holy Spirit's power can keep a single person from fornication?

_____
_____
_____
_____
_____
_____
_____
_____
_____
_____
_____
_____
_____
_____
_____
_____
_____
_____

Section 6

Your Vocation/Calling

After you were called to repentance and baptized with the Holy Spirit there should be a desire for growth and development to be of service in the kingdom of God. We are all called to serve and therefore, we must be equipped for any calling we have on our lives. No one is exempt because we are all ministers in the Body of Christ. Know your calling and operate in that position.

a.   Introduction

b.   The Holy Spirit

c.   Know your Calling

d.   Constancy

e.   Trust in God

f.   Lowliness and Meekness

a.   Longsuffering

b.   Love

c.   Unity of the Spirit

d.   The Bond of Peace

e.   Forgiveness

f.   Summary

_____

_____

_____

_____

Your Vocation/Calling
Lesson 1: Romans 4:13-25, II Peter 3

Introduction

Similar to natural gifts, every Child of God has a spiritual gift, talent, or calling [*vocation*], given by the Holy Spirit. Our calling is what we use to minister, for growth, and to bring souls into the Kingdom. We use this calling under the power, guidance, and inspiration of the Holy Spirit.

The Scriptures give clear instructions on how we are to use our calling, and described the way we should conduct ourselves. He did not list the gifts or direct us to any specific one. Instead, he showed us that as members of the Body of Christ we should do all in our power to keep unity and bind it up with peace. This does not mean only for outward appearance, but if we obey the instructions given, our behaviour will show the kind of persons we are.

In **Colossians 4:5**, we read, **Walk in wisdom toward them that are without, redeeming the time**. This is crisp and to the point language for the believer to adhere and obey. Each person is equipped with all that is necessary for the ministry. Listed below are some of the provision God has given His people to aid and enhance them in their walk with Him.

The Holy Spirit

It is not possible for any Christian to live a life of integrity without the work and presence of the Holy Spirit. The Holy Spirit is the only power upon earth, Who will enable us to do that which is right before God and man. The word teaches us to **walk in the Spirit**, [**Galatians 5:16, 24**], and this is the only way we can live a life that is creditable, and which God can remark favourably about us as He did with Job [**Job 2:3**].

Know your Calling

What is your calling? What is your purpose and worth in the Body of Christ? We are members of one Body, with Jesus Christ as the head. Each member has something to do, and that ministry/job is your calling. It is your spiritual vocation in the Body of Christ. The calling is a gift or gifts given and operated by the demonstration of the Holy Spirit who gives to every one as He wills [**II Corinthians 12:11**].

Paul delineated the purpose for each gift we receive in **Ephesians 4:12**. Whatever the gift is, the purpose is for the glory of God.

Steadfastness

Ephesians 4:1-3]

I therefore, the prisoner of the Lord, beseech you that ye walk worthy of the vocation wherewith ye are called, [1]

With all lowliness and meekness, with longsuffering, forbearing one another in love; [2]

Endeavouring to keep the unity of the Spirit in the bond of peace, [3]

Clearly then, we have a duty to maintain true spirituality in all that we do, and the way we interact with those around us. We cannot live one way six days of the week and a different way on Sundays. If we live like this, we become chameleons or animals who change according to situation. God does not want us to be deceptive or dishonest. We must live the way that describes the holiness of the God we claim to serve. To walk worthy, **first** means to <u>value</u> our calling by living a life that is pleasing to bring honour to His holy name.

Second, our life must be commendable, admirable, and worthwhile with an earnestness to fulfill the requirements our calling demands. Sometimes we get weary and lose focus, but Paul gave us instructions to be faithful in order to maintain constancy.

He noted, **Therefore, my beloved brethren, be ye steadfast, unmoveable, always abounding in the work of the Lord, forasmuch as ye know that your labour is not in vain in the Lord, [I Corinthians 15:58].**

And let us not be weary in well doing: for in due season we shall reap, if we faint not, [Gal. 6:9].

Trust in God

Building trust in any relationship requires faith and confidence in that individual. Trust means there is reliance upon God to keep His promises. In **Proverbs 3:5-6**, we read, **Trust in the Lord with all thine heart; and lean not unto thine own understanding. In all thy ways acknowledge him, and he shall direct thy paths.** We can put our trust in God no matter what the circumstances might be. God does not fail and has never proven to fail.

According to the word, **God is not a man, that he should lie; neither the son of man, that he should repent: hath he said, and shall he not do it? Or hath he spoken, and shall he not make it good? [Numbers 23:19]** God cannot lie, nor will He go back on His word.

Further, in **Isaiah 55:8-11]**, the passage states, **For as the rain comes down, and the snow from heaven, and returns not thither, but waters the earth, and makes it bring forth and bud, that it may give seed to the sower, and bread to the eater: [10]**

So shall my word be that goes forth out of my mouth: it shall not return unto me void, but it shall accomplish that which I please, and it shall prosper (*in the thing*) whereto I sent it. [11]

Trust in the Lord for ever: for in the Lord Jehovah is everlasting strength, [Isaiah 26:4].

If we have confidence in God, it leads to spiritual integrity. It demonstrates security and assurance in our relationship with Him. Even when we have problems or our prayers seem long in obtaining an answer we will wait upon God who cannot fail.

Lowliness and Meekness

In the world today, many are always seeking for "rights" and "fairness." There is nothing wrong with seeking equity and justice. However, there are times when we have to give way to wrath and let God perform the work of vengeance [Romans 12:9-21].

Even when we know that we deserve better treatment from others, we must still maintain spiritual decorum that will show dignity with modesty and tact. Let God fight for you because He knows exactly what to do. We often do things and later regret our actions. However, when we leave things in God's hands He takes over and we have the victory.

Lowliness and meekness speaks of humility. In Micah 6:8 we read, He has shown thee O man, what is good; and what does the Lord require of thee, but to do justly, and to love mercy, and to walk humbly with thy God?

One of the signs of humility is giving way to others, and not taking glory from God. It is modesty with an attitude of unselfish concern for the welfare and feelings of others. There is no conceit or arrogance, nor is there a spirit of competiveness.

Integrity

The person of integrity learns to wait upon God for answers to prayer. The word teaches us, But they that wait upon the Lord shall renew their strength; they shall mount up with wings as eagles; they shall run, and not be weary; and they shall walk, and not faint, [Isaiah 40:31].

Psalm 27:14, teaches us, Wait on the Lord: be of good courage, and he shall strengthen thine heart: wait, I say, on the Lord.

Moreover, we are further encouraged, For since the beginning of the world men have not heard, nor perceived by the ear, neither hath the eye seen, O God, beside thee, what he hath prepared for him that waits for him, [Isaiah 64:4].

There is no shame in waiting upon God because He does not disappoint those who put their trust in Him. The word said, for they shall not be ashamed that wait for the Lord, [Isaiah 49:23b].

And hope makes not ashamed; because the love of God is shed abroad in our hearts by the Holy Ghost which is given unto us, [Romans 5:5].

If our confidence in God is strong, we can say like the writer, **For the Lord God will help me; therefore shall I not be confounded: therefore have I set my face like a flint, and I know that I shall not be ashamed, [Isaiah 50:7].** This is integrity speaking because of faithfulness and trust in a God who cannot fail. See also **Isaiah 54:4.**

In order to keep integrity, we must show spiritual morals of honesty, truthfulness, reliability, and uprightness. Others' must be able to trust our word, once given that we will follow through with promises. Otherwise, no one will want to trust us. The demonstration of our calling is vital to the portrayal of Jesus Christ in our lives. If we are not sincere, or we tarnish our character with sin, we will only show the world a false image of Christianity. Sinfulness does not relate to the graces in fruits of the Spirit [**Galatians 5:22-23**]. Moreover, the person who maintains integrity will not surrender under pressure no matter what the situation might be.

Job was an example of integrity [**Job 2:1-3**] whom God recognized as a person of strong and endurable faith.

Abraham waited for God to fulfill His promise to him even though it took so many years after Ishmael for Isaac to be born [**Genesis 21**]. Despite the length of time, God kept His promise, while Abraham patiently waited for Him. During the time of waiting, Abraham held on to his faith and trust in God [**Romans 4:13-25**]. This is another example of integrity no matter what forces are against us.

David was anointed king of Israel, but he became a fugitive for years before he could assume the throne. Nevertheless, he did not neglect his duty to serve God and to hold on to his integrity knowing that God's word is true, [**Psalm 12:6-7**].

The person of integrity will not cheat on a spouse. Love is vital for anyone who seeks to please God and it must be with sincerity. It makes no sense trying to pretend that we love someone when deep in our hearts we really do not care for the individual.

Love must be sincere, and it must be feelings, which makes us sensitive to the feelings of others [**Romans 12:9**]. We must be kind, with love as the guiding principle shown to everyone with whom we interact. It might not always be easy to express, but with God, through the Holy Spirit we can do all things [**Philippians 4:13**].

The Bond of Peace

The word of God teaches, **Thou wilt keep him in perfect peace whose heart is stayed on Him**, [Isaiah 26:3]. We experience peace with God when we obey His word.

According to the word of God, **But the meek shall inherit the earth; and shall delight themselves in the abundance of peace, [Psalm 37:11].** We cannot produce the fruit of peace if we are constantly at war with each other. To enjoy peace or to keep the bond of peace, the Bible teaches, **Depart from evil, and do good; seek peace, and pursue it, [Psalm 34:14].** Peace, similar to love, must be expressed in practical ways. Jesus said, **Blessed are the peacemakers; for they shall be called the children of God**, [Matthew 5:9, *See also* II Timothy 2:24-26].

Forgiveness [Matthew 5:43-48, 6:14-15, Mark 11:25-26, Romans 12:9-21]

In closing, we cannot leave this section without looking at the spirit of forgiveness. All of us face trials and troubles, sometimes caused by or contributed by the behaviours of others. When we get hurt, the tendency is to protect ourselves from further discomfort. We protect ourselves in various ways even when the method is not right.

As people of God, we must demonstrate Christian values depicting qualities of Jesus Christ. **Let us not forget that the word Christian means "Christ-likeness."** These qualities cause others to recognize differences in our lives when compared to sinners.

Those Christ-like behaviours show the transforming work of the Holy Spirit, which make us different. However, with the demonstration of forgiveness, we will seek peace rather than carry the burden of a grudge on our shoulders.

According to the word of God, **Dearly beloved, avenge not yourselves, but rather give place unto wrath: for it is written, Vengeance is mine: I will repay, saith the Lord, [Romans 12:19].**

Earlier in the passage, it tells us to, **Recompense to no man evil for evil. Provide things honest in the sight of all men**, [Romans 12:17].

This shows the importance of letting go and forgiving for God to handle our problems. He, through the Holy Spirit will give us the right methods, set the right time, and the right circumstances for us to handle every situation, which comes into our lives. No situation is impossible for God to give us the right methods for resolving them.

Finally, we are encouraged by these words, **Be not overcome of evil, but overcome evil with good [Romans 12:21].** We must do everything in our power to make peace [**Romans 12:18**], and leave punishment to God who has wisdom to deal with anything. Show kindness instead of retribution and malice. It is always better to give way rather than seek for revenge.

_____

_____

_____

Your Vocation/Calling

Summary

The main theme of this section is steadfastness to our calling. This must be the symbol in the life of every believer. It requires faithfulness and integrity, which means honesty, truthfulness, reliability, commitment, and sincerity. We demonstrate these in the way we portray ourselves as Christians. The requirements are spiritual graces reflecting the fruit of the Spirit such as love, joy, meekness, patience, love, and peace. We are on stage and in the market place of the world every day. People are looking on, and they expect to see something worthwhile in us by the way we behave. Somebody is seeking for something better in life, and your life may be the only picture that is set before that individual. Let us remain faithful to our calling so that the end we shall hear **well done, thou good, and faithful servant. Enter into the joy of thy Father.**

Suggestions for further reading

I Corinthians 15:58

Galatians 6:7-10

I Thessalonians 3:4

Discussion
   i.   What does it means to have a calling on one's life?
   ii. Do you know your calling, and are you operating in it?
   iii. Do you think pastors should accept anyone who comes with a burning calling on his or her life, yet the individual does not seem serious about serving the Lord?
   iv. Should leaders forbid anyone for operating in his or her calling?
   v.   What might happen to someone who refuses to assume the calling on his or her life?

_____
_____
_____
_____
_____
_____
_____
_____
_____

Section 7

God's Protective Power

Every parent takes care of his family and so does God to His people. He loves us, and watches over us. Furthermore, He tells us in His word that He is jealous **[Exodus 20:5, Deuteronomy 5:9],** and will not share us with anyone else. This type of emotion is not in the negative sense, but He wants us to know that He cares about us more than even a mother over her child. God named Himself Jealous, stating, **For thou shalt worship no other god: the Lord, whose name is Jealous, is a jealous God, [Exodus 34:14].** He is saying that He does not want any competition because He can give us all that we need. His complete provision for us is sufficient to prevent us from going after other gods. He <u>watches</u> over us, <u>guides</u> us, <u>teaches</u> and <u>protects</u> us. Even when we stray from His loving arms, He seeks us out, and if we return, He receives us with open arms **[Isaiah 55].**

This section will discuss five aspects of God's protective power towards His people.

    a. He gives us Peace

    b. He gives us His Great Love

    c. He gives us Salvation

    d. He Disciplines Us

    e. He gives us His Word

_____

_____

_____

_____

_____

God's Protective Power

Psalm 91, 121

Introduction

Deuteronomy 31:6, 8

Be strong and of a good courage, fear not, nor be afraid of them: for the Lord thy God, he it is that doth go with thee; he will not fail thee, nor forsake thee. [6]

And the Lord, he it is that doth go before thee; he will be with thee, he will not fail thee, neither forsake thee: fear not, neither be dismayed. [8]

Psalm 91

He that dwells in the secret place of the most High shall abide under the shadow of the Almighty. [1]

There shall no evil befall thee, neither shall any plague come nigh thy dwelling. [10]

For he shall give his angels charge over thee, to keep thee in all thy ways. [11]

They shall bear thee up in their hands, lest thou dash thy foot against a stone. [12]

Isaiah 54:17

No weapon that is formed against thee shall prosper; and every tongue that shall rise against thee in judgment, thou shalt condemn. This is the heritage of the servants of the Lord, and their righteousness is of me saith the Lord.

God's care for His people goes beyond our human understanding [**Psalm 103**]. It expands to all generations and will continue until the Lord Jesus puts in His appearance to take His Bride away. In **Deuteronomy 33:12**, we read, **The beloved of the Lord shall dwell in safety by him; and the Lord shall cover him all the day long, and he shall dwell between his shoulders.**

This passage reflects the permanent continuous watchfulness of God's eyes over His people. Safety means being securely protected. You have confidence that God will not leave you unprotected to the wolfish situations in the world or the lion-like nature of the enemy who is always on the prowl.

God's Protective Power

God is always near [**Psalm 46:1**] to protect us, and constantly stands guard like a sentinel around us. When we call upon Him in our times of trouble, He not only hears, but He answers us.

Psalm 121: 3-7ff, He will not suffer thy foot to be moved: he that keeps thee will not slumber. Behold, he that keeps Israel shall neither slumber nor sleep. The Lord is thy keeper: the Lord is thy shade upon thy right hand. The sun shall not smite thee by day, nor the moon by night. The Lord shall preserve thee from all evil. There is no one on earth who can give this kind of constant protection, **twenty-four hours daily, seven days weekly,** but God.

God is a preserver and constant protector of His people. We do not have to fear because He does not get weary. He is watching over us all day long. He covers us with His protective power and shields us from danger. Even when we are face to face with the enemy, we may suffer bruises in battle, but we will always be the winner.

God covers His people with His presence and gives us safety from the enemy who daily seeks to persecute us. Moreover, when we make God Lord of our lives, the word tells us, **Thou shalt not be afraid for the terror by night; nor for the arrow that flies by day; nor for the pestilence that walks in darkness; nor for the destruction that wastes at noonday... Only with thine eyes shalt thou behold and see the reward of the wicked,** [**Psalm 91:5-8**].

Each passage is an encouragement to the child of God who seeks to please Him and to obey His word. We are fully encouraged that we have no need to fear; rather we are to trust in God who will not fail us. He sends His angels to keep guard over us all the time.

When we acknowledge God's protective power, we will safely and confidently, rest in Him [**Psalm 37:7**]. We will wait upon His will for our life. Moreover, we will confidently and boldly, **hope** as we patiently wait; knowing that we are constantly under His watchful eyes; and covered by the Blood of Jesus Christ.

Discussion

i. If God really cares about us, and watches over us 24/7, why do we wait so long for answers to our prayers?

ii. What are some ways in which God protects His people, even when He does not answer some of our prayers?

iii. Why do you think God does not answer all of our prayers when He hears every one of them?

iv. Why does God stands by when we are in trouble and pain, and seems to do nothing?

v. What should the believer do when God is silent?

Lesson 1: Methods of Protection [a]

Isaiah 26:3-4, 55:6-7, Hebrews 12:5-11

Introduction

God protects us in many ways by giving us various weapons to use against the enemy who tries to distract or mislead us. Those weapons are not only for protection, but also for warfare.

God's protective power gives us *peace*, *consolation*, and *contentment* so that we are able to trust Him under any situation. God's peace keeps us from worry and fear. It directs our mind away from things, which will cause us to murmur and complain. Instead, we trust in God and depend on His loving-kindnesses and mercies.

If we keep our minds on the Lord, His peace will saturate our heart and mind [**Isaiah 26:3-4, Philippians 4:7**]. Jesus Christ brought peace by breaking down the walls between God and us [**Ephesians 2:14**]. When God's peace resides in our hearts, there will be no place for anxiety, which often leads to stress and depression. We will not feel at any time that God has forsaken or abandoned us because we trust in Jehovah who is our *refuge*, *strength*, *guide*, and *protector*.

God's Great Love

We read in the Bible that God sent His only begotten Son into the world to die for our sins, because of His great love towards mankind [**John 3:16**]. Still, how often do we think of God being a loving Father? God so loved the world, shows a love, which is incomparable to any kind of love we have ever known, or will ever know. This love is remarkable, unchangeable, and unceasing. Even when we sin and later turn to God for His forgiveness, He is willing and ready to forgive the penitent who seeks Him [**Psalm 86:5**]. God's love for mankind should make each one of us love one another; especially those who are of the Christian faith should express love without reservation. We did not do anything good to deserve God's Son. We did not inherit this love from Him through our parents. Instead, this love He gives freely to those who will accept it.

One reason we can think of why God sent His only Son into the world to die for sinners is to protect us from eternal damnation. If the Lord Jesus had not come, we would all, be eternally separated from God because of inherited sin from Adam.

There are two important features about God's love towards us

The first is that this love is not partial. He calls everyone [**John 3:16-17**], and turns away no one. God is love not only in Spirit, but also in practicality. He planted His love into our hearts. [**Romans 5:5**], states, **The love of God is shed abroad in our hearts by the Holy Ghost which is given unto us.**

Second, God's love is unconditional because He sent His Son in a world of sin to die for sinners.

In [**Romans 5:6-8**] we read that, **For when we were yet without strength, in due time Christ died for the ungodly. For scarcely for a righteous man will one die...But God commended his love toward us, in that, while we were yet sinners, Christ died for us.** This passage sums up the depth, breath, and height: the total dimensions of God's great love for us. God's love toward us is incomprehensible.

Moreover, God had great compassion for us, to extend His mercy beyond our sins through forgiveness.

It took unconditional love to bring us to a saving grace in Jesus Christ. Furthermore, the Bible teaches that love covers a multitude of sins [**I Peter 4:8**]. Clearly then, God's love gives us protection, not just to cover our sins, but also to forgive us from all unrighteousness.

Still, although this love is free, yet there are those who do not see the necessity of accepting Jesus Christ as their indwelling personal Saviour. Many do not believe that He is God's Son. However, to **as many who believe and receive Him, to them gave He power to become the sons of God** [John 1:12-13].

Accepting Jesus Christ in our lives restores the protection we once had before the fall of man in the Garden of Eden. God's love gives us protection and makes us secure and firm in the knowledge that He cares for us.

The Gift of Salvation

Salvation comes through the redemptive work of Jesus Christ. Originally, we were all born in sin [**Psalm 51:5, Behold, I was shapen in iniquity; and in sin did my mother conceive me**]; with the sinful nature [**Romans 3:10, As it is written, 'There is none righteous, no, not one**]. Being born with a sinful nature, made us sin by choice [**Romans 3:23, For all have sinned, and come short of the glory of God**].

In **Ephesians 2:1-8**, we read that the grace of God brought salvation through faith. We have salvation, which means redemption from eternal death.

Although we were dead in sin, we became alive through Jesus Christ's death, burial, and resurrection. We now have hope of eternal life. Each person has an opportunity for salvation by accepting Jesus Christ, God's Son through water baptism, and the infilling of the Holy Spirit [**John 3**].

Salvation is free, and we receive this by grace through faith in Jesus Christ. All have the opportunity to receive Jesus by believing that He is the Son of God. No one is omitted, and no one who accepts Him will be turned away. In **John 1:12** we read, **But as many as received him, to them gave he power to become the sons of God, even to them that believe on his name.**

Discipline

God's discipline is a spiritual method He uses to keep us in obedience because He loves us **[Job 5:17, Proverbs 3:10-11]**. It is also for *spiritual growth*, *maturity*, *training* and *strength*. The word says, **He opens also their ear to discipline, and commands that they return from iniquity, [Job 36:10].** It means that He will use chastisement, correction, and instruction because discipline is beneficial to us. The word further states in **Hebrews 12:5-6, 8-11:**

And ye have forgotten the exhortation which speaks unto you as unto children, My son, despise not thou the chastening of the Lord, nor faint when thou art rebuked of him: [5]

For whom the Lord loves he chastens, and scourges every son whom he receives. [6]

But if ye be without chastisement, whereof all are partakers, then are ye bastards, and not sons. [8]

Furthermore we have had fathers of our flesh which corrected (us), and we gave them reverence: shall we not much rather be in subjection unto the Father of spirits, and live? [9]

For they verily for a few days chastened (*us*) after their own pleasure; but he for (*our*) profit, that we might be partakers of his holiness. [10]

Now no chastening for the present seems to be joyous, but grievous: nevertheless afterward it yields the peaceable fruit of righteousness unto them which are exercised thereby. [11]

_____
_____
_____
_____
_____
_____
_____
_____
_____
_____
_____
_____
_____
_____

Lesson 2: Methods of Protection [b]

Hebrews 12:5-11

_____

The Word of God

Hebrews 4:12, For the word of God is quick, and powerful, and sharper than any two-edged sword, piercing even to the dividing asunder of soul and spirit, and of the joints and marrow, and is a discerner of the thoughts and intents of the heart.

Psalm 12:6, The words of the Lord are pure words: as silver is tried in a furnace of earth, purified seven times.

Word: *lógos*, the expression of speech; to speak prophetically. A saying or discourse.
Quick: *zaō*, to have life
Diving asunder: *merismós*, distribution
Soul: *psuché*, the immaterial part of man in common with animals. It is the element of life, and refers to man's fallen nature and his sinfulness.
Spirit: *pneúma*, the invisible part of man, which gives him the ability to think on God.
Discerner: *kritikós*, to judge, determine, make decision
Intents: *énnoia*, purpose

Hebrews 12:5-11, tells us about God's discipline, and why He does it. God reminds us that our earthly fathers discipline us mostly for their own pleasure, but He does it because of His love, and considers us His children. The passage tells us that if we are not disciplined, then are we bastards and therefore, do not belong into the family of God. Discipline is necessary, and none of us should try to escape, nor should any one rebel against God's discipline [**II Timothy 4:2**].

Through Suffering

The Christian life is one of service unto the Lord, which will always include some type of suffering. We cannot go through the experience without understanding this important factor concerning the Christian life. Jesus suffered the just for the unjust. He paid a great price for our salvation. The only way we can know Jesus or even begin to relate to Him, is by going through the experience of suffering. Paul noted in his writings, **That I may know him; and the power of his resurrection, and the fellowship of his sufferings, being made conformable unto his death**, [**Philippians 3:10**].

We go through suffering for one of two reasons. We suffer either because of our **disobedience**; or for the Lord through **persecution [I Peter 4:7-19]**. There are times when we do wrong or we disobey God, and He disciplines us. The discipline may also be God's way for showing His love of protection so that we do not go astray from Him. God sometimes allows situations to occur in our lives so that we learn to depend upon Him.

Suffering requires *self-control, patience, willingness, self-sacrifice, obedience, trust, faithfulness,* and *selflessness*. Moreover, from the day, we accept the Lord Jesus Christ; the enemy marks us, and becomes a tyrant and adversary against us. None of us is unique to suffering because Jesus Christ suffered. Therefore, we will endure suffering for His sake to show our love and appreciation for what He did for us on Calvary. According to the word, **Count it all joy when ye fall into divers temptations; knowing this, that the trying of your faith works patience. But let patience have her perfect work, that ye may be entire, wanting nothing, [James 1:1-2]**.

God's Constant Care

God keeps a watchful eye over us every day all through the day. The reason why He does this is in the word where He said, **I the Lord thy God am a Jealous God, [Exodus 20]**.

God is passionate about His people and cares about their welfare every day. His jealousy is not fanaticism. Rather, it is sincere concern so that we do not return to the sinful life we lived before accepting Him in our hearts.

God is faithful to His people and He expects the same from us, and that we give reverence to His name.

In the Commandments God specifically warns us against idolatry, **[Exodus 20:1-5]**. God's care for us is intense, which means we can rest securely under His protective power.

Consequently, God's care for us depicts what His name represents "Jealous" to watch over and protect us [Psalm 23]. We belong to Him and He seals His ownership by adopting us into His family through Jesus Christ [Romans 8].

_____

_____

_____

_____

_____

_____

_____

Lesson 3: Methods of Protection [c]

Romans 12:1-2, Galatians 5:16, 24, James 4:7

The Holy Spirit

John 14:16, And I will pray the Father, and he shall give you another Comforter, that he may abide with you forever.

Even the Spirit of truth; whom the world cannot receive, because it sees him not, neither knows him: but ye know him; for he dwells with you, and shall be in you. [17]

Further, we read in **Luke 10:19**, where Jesus gave the disciples power over serpents, scorpions and over all the power of the enemy. This power comes from the Holy Spirit.

With the concept of power, two thoughts come to mind – authority and force. We have the **authority** to cast out demons and make them subject to us [**Matthew 10:1**].

We have **power** over the works of Satan and his force. Jesus did not only give the disciples power against unclean spirits, but to heal all manner of diseases. This power and authority works through us by the Holy Spirit and not because of a title or position an individual holds.

Many people desire the power and authority, but do not want to face the challenges of living holy in order to be effective. To be effective, we must submit to God and the leading of the Holy Spirit if He controls our life.

Weapons of Warfare

God protects us by bestowing gifts to us so that we can face the trials, which we will experience in our walk as Christians.

The gifts of the Spirit are diverse for various administrations and operations. They manifest themselves in various forms in the Body of Christ [**I Corinthians 12:4-6**], and as weapons against the enemy [**II Corinthians 10:3-6**]. [See **I Corinthians 12, Ephesians 4, and Romans 12**] for gifts of the Spirit.

The encounters we face are often demonic situations working through individuals and circumstances to cause us distresses [**Ephesians 6:12-18**].

Discussion

i.   How can we use spiritual weapons to fight the trials of life when they come through <u>individuals</u> and <u>institutions</u>?

ii. Does God really cares when our hearts are broken and there is no one to help?

iii. If God is a **"present help in the time of trouble"** why do we have to wait so long? Why does He not answer when we need Him most?

iv. Can you explain why God disciplines His people?

v.   If God loves His people, why does He allow them to go through suffering, some of which are extremely severe?

vi. Do you think it is necessary for believers to suffer, even when they are faithful to God?

Section 8

False Teachers

False teachers are just what it says "false" which means they are deceitful, insincere, and dishonest, with many other labels to describe them. Paul warned that in the last days **some will depart from the faith, giving heed to seducing spirits, and doctrines of devils: Speaking lies in hypocrisy; having their conscience seared with a hot iron, [I Timothy 4:1-2]**. He did not stop there, but encouraged leaders stating, **If thou put the brethren in remembrance of these things, thou shalt be a good minister of Jesus Christ, nourished up in the words of faith and of good doctrine, whereunto thou hast attained, [I Timothy 4:6]**.

The topic for this section includes the following:

a. Introduction

b. Description of False Teachers

c. False Teachers are Dangerous

d. Their Destruction End

_____
_____
_____
_____
_____
_____
_____
_____
_____
_____

False Teachers

Lesson 1: II Peter 2:1-22, Jude 1-25

Introduction

Peter took the time to warn us of heretics who are destructive to the work of the Lord, and the doctrines as was introduced by Jesus. Those persons are not careful with their interpretation of God's word; and they use any types of excuses to validate their arrogance. Nevertheless, the Bible states that, **Whosoever transgresses, and abides not in the doctrine of Christ, hath not God. He that abides in the doctrine of Christ, he hath both the Father and the Son**, [II John 9].

When someone departs from the word of truth, this is a spirit of rebellion against God. That person no longer obeys the word, but does whatever he or she pleases.

They are defiant and walk in their disobedience [**Romans 1:21-23, 28-32**]. The Bible states, **He that says he abides in him ought himself also so to walk, even as he walked**, [I John 1:6]. Consequently, if the individual is not walking in the principles laid down for Christianity, he or she is living a lie.

Earlier in the passage it says, **He that says I know him, and keeps not his commandments, is a liar, and the truth is not him**, [I John 1:4]. These are evidences, which will prove our faithfulness to the faith or not.

There are many ways in which heretics use their unscriptural beliefs to sell their products, one of which is to preface their teachings with their intellectual and humanistic knowledge.

The mistake followers make in believing heretics is in agreeing with them and accepting their theories, which oppose the true meaning and interpretation of God's word.

Despite their weakness and vulnerability, weak Christians do not have to remain in a fallen condition. There is hope and forgiveness, if and when, we sin [**I John 1:7-2:2**].

_____

_____

_____

_____

False Teachers

Lesson 2: Description of False Teachers

II Timothy 3:2-9, II Peter 2:10-13

Introduction

The Bible calls them "...**spots and blemishes, having eyes full of adultery, and that cannot cease from sin; beguiling unstable souls...**" [Jude 13-14].

Wells without water, clouds that are carried with a tempest; to whom the mist [gloom] of darkness is reserved for ever, [II Peter 2:17].

These natural brute beasts, made to be taken and destroyed, speak evil of the things that they understand not; and shall utterly perish in their own corruption; And shall receive the reward of unrighteousness, as they that count it pleasure to riot in the day time, [II Peter 2:10-13].

Sinful Devilish Behaviour

False teachers are devilish in their behaviour. According to the word, **He that commits sin is of the devil; for the devil sinned from the beginning. For this purpose the Son of God was manifested, that he might destroy the works of the devil**, [I John 3:8].

Self-willed

Indeed, those leaders who teach that all marital constructs are acceptable are false teachers. There is no question about the truth of God's word if we take heed.

The Scripture is clear which states, **Knowing this first, that no prophecy of the Scripture is of any private interpretation. For the prophecy came not in old time by the will of man: but holy men of God spoke as they were moved by the Holy Ghost**, [II Peter 1:20-21]. Not only are they self-willed but there are selfish because they only to please themselves, [**II Timothy 3:2-9**].

Those who believe it is all right to marry someone from the same gender and still consider himself, herself to be a Christian is lying to the self. Peter said they will **bring upon themselves swift destruction**, [II Peter 2:1]

Carnal

The false teacher may not only live an immoral life, but is carnal by giving way to lusts and all manner of sexual uncleanness [**II Peter 2:10**].

Including are leaders who are abusers and whose wives live in fear of them. Those wives endure the physical and emotional attacks because they may be afraid of their husbands.

Not only do those leaders abuse their wives but they also abuse church members, all in the Name of Christianity.

_____

_____

_____

_____

_____

_____

_____

_____

_____

_____

_____

_____

_____

_____

_____

_____

_____

_____

_____

_____

_____

_____

Lesson 3: Self-Titled Leaders

II Peter 2:18-19ff

Modern Day Prophets

The **first** set of title holders are the present day prophets. Over the years, I came across people who called themselves Christians displaying various forms of religions and Christian disciplines. However, I really do not recall hearing of or meeting so many who are prophets, and apostles. It seems to be the new craze in the church community.

I mean, they are popping up like weeds everywhere without control. There are pastors who *make* their wives prophets. True! What is going on? Is it any wonder that each of those prophets only has a prosperity message and nothing else? Are any of those persons hearing from God? Have they ever heard from God? Do they really know God; not of Him, do they *know* Him?

Those want-to-be prophets speak from their spiritually sick minds to make the gullible feel good. God is against such prophets because they lie by using His name. They are deceivers who **creep into houses, and lead captive silly women laden with sins, led away with divers lusts, (II Timothy 3:6)**.

Jude went deeply in describing deceivers stating, **For there are certain men crept in unawares, who were before of old ordained to this condemnation, ungodly men, turning the grace of our God into lasciviousness, and denying the only Lord God, and our Lord Jesus Christ, [Jude 4]**.

These self-titled want-to-be "officials", use Christianity as a veil to cover their falsehood; cannot be trusted. If the veil was lifted, you will find that spiritual treason is being committed each time they open their mouths.

A true prophet does not ask for money or payment, which is a sure sign of spiritual fraud because it is being done under the guise of Christianity. Those persons are liars and thieves. They are not working for the Lord. They are no different from the palm-readers and such like. At least they do not pretend to be Christians.

These are the Jezebels, who are in the churches stifling growth and preventing the flow of the Holy Spirit. In fact, He withdraws from them. Those persons prophesy in **their** name, and not in the Name of Jesus.

Modern Day Apostles

The **second** observation of note, are the "apostles" of today. My, my, my, these too are floating everywhere and there seem to be no stopping them. Everyone wants to be a title-holder even if it means just having a "certain" title to precede introductions.

In **Revelation 2:2**, Jesus said, **Thou hast tried them which say they are apostles, and are not, and hast found them liars.** What is this thing about titles? Who are those persons trying to impress?

Paul stated, **For such are false apostles, deceitful workers, transforming themselves into the apostles of Christ, [II Corinthians 11:13].**

False Teachers are Dangerous

For when they speak great swelling (*words*) of vanity, they allure through the lusts of the flesh, (*through much*) wantonness, those that were clean escaped from them who live in error.

While they promise them liberty, they themselves are the servants of corruption: for of whom a man is overcome, of the same is he brought in bondage, [II Peter 2:18-19ff].

Peter noted that those greedy persons promise liberty [from poverty if they send to the ministry], but they are servants of corruption [**II Peter 2:19**].

Peter shows us that false teachers are not new. They have been around before even as they are today. One of the dangers is that they use the media to expound and sell their destructive doctrines, which may sound like the right thing, but when matched with the word of God, has no power. Peter warned that they do their work secretly and cunningly so that, unless the listener is open to the Holy Spirit, he or she can be easily deceived.

False teachers are dangerous because their behaviour characterizes the church in a negative manner, and others are hurt and penalized by their wicked actions. Those conducts affect church attendance and giving to local pastors who are truly teaching God's word.

According to **II Peter 2:3**, **Through covetousness shall they with feigned words make merchandise of you.** How true are these words? Those persons use deception and guile to sneak into the hearts of weak people to encourage them to give because it is unto the Lord's work. They use those funds to make themselves rich so that they can live the easy life while you continue to struggle. Yes, they are conniving, evil, and wicked. As the word says, they make merchandise of those who are spiritually weak and blind. They exploit people and then leave them when they are in trouble.

Jude made mention of them in his writing stating, **Woe unto them! For they have gone in the way of Cain, and ran greedily after the error of Balaam for reward, and perished in the gainsaying of Core... [Jude 11-13].**

Lesson 4: Their Destructive End

II Peter 2:4-9, 13

There is no Escape

II Peter 2:4-9

If God spared not the angels that sinned, but cast them down to hell, and delivered them into chains of darkness, to be reserved unto judgment; [4]

And spared not the old world, but saved Noah the eighth person, a preacher of righteousness, bringing in the flood upon the world of the ungodly, [5]

And turning the cities of Sodom and Gomorrah into ashes condemned them with an overthrow, (*making*) them an ensample unto those that after should live ungodly. [6]

And delivered just Lot, vexed with the filthy conversation of the wicked: [7]

(For that righteous man dwelling among them, in seeing and hearing, vexed his righteous soul from day to day with their unlawful deeds;) [8]

The Lord knows how to deliver the godly out of temptations, and to reserve the unjust unto the day of judgment to be punished: [9]

_____

_____

_____

_____

_____

_____

_____

II Peter 2:20-22

For if after they have escaped the pollutions of the world through the knowledge of the Lord and Saviour Jesus Christ, they are again entangled therein, and overcome, the latter end is worse with them than the beginning. [20]

For it had been better for them not to have known the way of righteousness, than, after they have known it, to turn from the holy commandment delivered unto them. [21]

But it has happened unto them according to the true proverb, 'The dog is turned to his own vomit again; and the sow that was washed to her wallowing in the mire,' [22]

The Bible tells us that, **Evil men and seducers shall wax worse and worse, deceiving, and being deceived,** [II Timothy 3:13].

The Just is Encouraged and Delivered

First, those who live godly are encouraged to **Continue in the things which you have learned and has been assured of, knowing of whom you have learned them,** [II Timothy 3:14].

Secondly, God will deliver the just before He brings judgment to those who do not observe His word, but live to please themselves. **The Lord knows how to deliver the godly out of temptations, and to reserve the unjust unto the day of judgment to be punished,** [II Peter 2:9].

Suggestions for further reading

a. Danger of false teachers: II Peter 2:1-4

b. Destruction of false teachers: 5-9, Jude 14-20

c. Description of false teachers: 10-22, Jude 5-11

_____

_____

_____

_____

_____

_____

_____

_____

_____

_____

_____

Section 9

The Deceitfulness of Sin

When sin is finished it brings forth death **[James 1:15]**. Even sin has a pay day, **For the wages of sin is death: but the gift of God is eternal life through Jesus Christ our Lord, [Romans 6:23]**. From the Garden of Eden, God showed that there is penalty for willful sinning. **But of the tree of the knowledge of good and evil, thou shalt not eat of it: for in the day that thou eatest thereof thou shalt surely die, [Genesis 2:17]**.

a. Introduction

b. The Deceiver

c. The Fall of Man

d. Temptation

e. Sin's Destructive Nature

f. Sin's Remedy

g. Sin Brings Judgment

h. A Call to Repentance

_____
_____
_____
_____
_____
_____
_____

The Deceitfulness of Sin
Lesson 1: The Fall of Man
Genesis 3:1-21

Introduction

The word deceitful is from the root word deceit. It means *intrigue*, *hidden*, *false*, *dishonest*, *devious, misleading, lying*, and so forth. The deceiver will make believe he is a friend and therefore, cunningly gain respect and trust. While at the same time, he is devising ways to gain your trust in order to deceive. The aim is for you to give up your *secrets*, your *desires*, your *hopes*, you name it; the deceiver knows how to carry out his act **[Genesis 3:1-6]**. He is very calculative and subtle, and uses those traits to approach his victims.

Satan deceives and acts on people's weaknesses and needs. He works through the mind, circumstances and people to infiltrate the hearts and lives of the vulnerable and those who are defenseless. The word of God tells us, **Thou wilt keep (*him*) in perfect peace, (*whose*) mind is stayed (*on thee*): because he trusts in thee, [Isaiah 26:3].** When we trust in God, and keep in consistent relationship with Him, we can overcome the enemy and not fall for his schemes.

We need to remind each other of the deceitfulness of sin. We must provoke one another to live holy. The word of God teaches us to, **Exhort one another daily, while it is called "To day;" lest any of you be hardened through the deceitfulness of sin**, [Hebrews 3:13].

When the heart gets hardened, it is the result of unbelief and this leads to departing from the truth to apostasy. This is why it is so important to stay in the word, and to be a regular/active member of a local church. Those who live ungodly lives only give a couple hours on a Sunday, but the balance of the week is for the service of the enemy.

_____
_____
_____

The Deceiver

In the Garden of Eden, the enemy used deceit to gain entrance into Eve's trust so that he could carry out his plan against mankind. His main mode of operation is to use the **senses** to gain attention.

For example, Eve saw that the fruit was desirable; then, she touched, and finally tasted it. The enemy tempted Eve, who yielded as her senses gave way to desire, even though the object of interest was forbidden. She immediately forgot the command from God and fell into sin. It did not end there, because she involved her husband Adam, who also became weak with what he saw and tasted.

Yet, it is all intrigue and guile, but it is deadly. Sin uses conspiracy, deception, schemes, charm, and plots **to captivate** and **allure** its victim whose interests have faded from walking after godliness.

The **deceitfulness** of sin is treachery and untrustworthiness including faithlessness because the individual, who once trusted God, has turned away from him and gone back to the beggarly elements. That person has committed spiritual adultery against his God, and no longer has the same love for him **[Revelation 2:4-5]**.

Features about Sin

There are many distinguishing features about sin, which should make every believer become aware of its character. Sin is **temptation**, which is destructive, and will eventually lead to death both spiritually and naturally. [**James 1:12-14**].

Nevertheless, although the enemy deceived Adam and Eve, he did not have similar result with the Lord Jesus when he tempted him **[Matthew 4:1-11]**. Jesus used **the word** to defeat the plan of the enemy. Therefore, the Scriptures admonished us to, **Let the word of Christ dwell in you in all wisdom; teaching and admonishing one another in psalms and hymns and spiritual songs, singing with grace in your hearts to the Lord, [Colossians 3:16].**

This means we should study, understand, memorize, and apply the word of God daily, so that we can overcome and defeat the plan of the enemy. He has all kinds of schemes with fiery darts, which he sends at our weakest moment, but we can be victors, and not casualties of his deceit.

Temptation leads to **lust**, which makes the weak person desire something forbidden [**James 1:15**]. In **Genesis 3:1-13**, we read of the fall of Man when the enemy used deceit to capture him into believing God had held back something important from him. The serpent [enemy] emphasized his point stating, **For God doth know that in the day ye eat thereof, then your eyes shall be opened, and ye shall be as gods, knowing good and evil [Genesis 3:5].** Immediately, interest was conceived; and, the quest for what this could be came into being. Consequently, man fell for something he thought was good for him; but which God had forbidden. Yet, the desire to have it was greater than obedience to God. This is where lust gives birth to sin: having the **wrong** desires.

Sin is **seductive**, and the enemy used all the methods of deceit to seduce the innocent couple, who fell for his sales pitch of lies and deception. Listen to him, Y**ea, hath God said, Ye shall not eat of every tree of the garden? [Genesis 3:1b]**. He is using the same theme today, and mankind is partaking of his delicacies, and being poisoned by the sin of disobedience, which is leading them to spiritual death.

Undoubtedly, Adam and Eve's hearts were set towards obedience; but they did not overcome the subtlety of the enemy, who was plotting their disobedience to God. Satan **hates** God and His people, and does everything to deceive.

Nevertheless, Jesus said, **Behold, I give unto you power to tread on serpents and scorpions, and over all the power of the enemy: and nothing shall by any means hurt you, [Luke 10:19]**. Therefore, the believer can overcome satanic attacks with the indwelling Holy Spirit, who gives power over the schemes of the enemy.

The Power of the Senses

When the woman saw that the tree (*was*) good for food, and that it (*was*) pleasant to the eyes, and a tree to be desired to make (*one*) wise, she took of the fruit thereof, and did eat, and gave also unto her husband with her; and he did eat, [Genesis 3:6].

There are three [3] salient concepts at work here relating to the senses: sight – seeing, attraction; taste – good for food and necessary; and intellect – knowledge, interest, perception.

This passage shows the significant role our senses play in the act of sin. It is the same today. There are perfumes, clothing, styles, and so on, which will attract and of course, mislead those who are careless in serving the Lord. Those things are not to improve our relationship with Him, but to bring us to a place of disobedience to His word. There is an allurement, which comes from the intrigue sin brings with its attempt to seduce the victim.

We have Needs

Sin also brings **passion** and **enticement**, with immediate desires to satisfy the flesh, causing many to fall easily into its trap.

The deceitfulness of sin will make the victim believes he is not doing wrong because he has needs that must be fulfilled. This is indeed true that we have needs, because we are not only of spirit: but spirit, soul, and body. We consist of immaterial elements [spirit and soul], and material substance, which is the body, **[I Thessalonians 5:23]**.

The spirit is that part of man, which communes with God, the soul incorporates the intellect, emotions, psyche, faculties, and so on, and the body is the encasement of spirit and soul. We can see the body, but not the other two elements. Therefore, we need all three to operate in concert so that the entire being is whole.

When taken out of context, someone might decide that I have to meet the needs of my body; otherwise, I might go crazy. You do not have to go crazy. This is a false impression the enemy gives you through deceit and fear.

Fig Leaves cannot Cover Sin

After Adam and Eve discovered their error, they saw themselves to be naked. Satan had gone about his business by then because he had accomplished his mission. He had no further use for them.

And the eyes of them both were opened, and they knew that they (*were*) naked; and they sewed fig leaves together, and made themselves aprons, [Genesis 3:7]. The <u>first mistake</u> the couple made was disobeying God. The <u>second</u> one was trying to cover their sin with fig leaves. Fig leaves cannot cover sin. The morning after tablet will not cover sin. A bath will not cover sin. Going to confession will not cover sin. The only covering, and cleansing for sin, is the **blood of Jesus Christ, [I John 1:16].**

During the last supper with the disciples, **Jesus took bread and blessed it, and broke it, and gave to his disciples, and said, Take, eat; this is my body. And he took the cup, and gave thanks, and gave it to them, saying, Drink ye all of it; For this is my blood of the new testament, which is shed for many for the remission of sins, [Matthew 26:26-28].** Only the Blood of Christ can cleanse sin.

There are **consequences** for sin. We see in **Genesis 3:14-21**, that God cursed the <u>enemy</u> [**Genesis 3:14-15**]; add sorrow to <u>the woman</u> with submissiveness to her husband [**Genesis 3:16**], sorrow and labour to <u>man</u> [**Genesis 3:17, 19**]; and cursed the <u>ground</u> [**Genesis 3:17-18**]. The price for sin is still great and no one escapes its consequences [**Romans 6:23**].

_____	**Suggestions for further reading**
_____	Genesis 3, 4, 6
_____	Psalm 38, 51
_____	James 1:12-18
_____	

_____

_____

_____

_____

_____

Lesson 2: Sin's Destructive Nature

Psalm 32:3-5, 38

Introduction

When David felt the heaviness of his sins, he sought forgiveness from God [**Psalm 51**]. There are times when we will pray to God about everything else, other than to seek forgiveness for our sinfulness. Yet, we come before Him seeking His presence in our ungodly state. God cannot tolerate sin, but He is ready and willing to forgive us of our sins [**Psalm 86:5**]. The word declares, **If we confess (*our*) sins, he is faithful and just to forgive us (*our*) sins, and to cleanse us from all unrighteousness, [I John 1:9].**

Sin Hurts

Sin is a condition, which affects us <u>socially</u>, <u>emotionally</u>, <u>physically</u>, and <u>spiritually</u>. We tend to hide when we commit sin because we do not want others to know about it. We become afraid and therefore, hide the sinfulness.

In **Psalm 38:6**, David said, **I am troubled; I am bowed down greatly: I go mourning all the day long. Psalm 38:3-6**, shows us the pressures of sin; how it affects even our bodies, and emotions. Sin has no pity; and will leave you weak and helpless. Sin causes emotional wounds, which smells each time you recall the memory. Sin takes away our health and our peace of mind. It nags and torments with no ease. It mocks and afflicts the sinner. If he tries to conceal it, sin will torment him.

Another time in **Psalm 32:3-5,** David said, **When I kept silence, my bones waxed old through my roaring all the day long. [3]**

For day and night thy hand was heavy upon me: my moisture is turned into the drought of summer. [4]

I acknowledge my sin unto thee, and mine iniquity have I not hid. I said, I will confess my transgressions unto the Lord; and thou forgave the iniquity of my sin. [5]

David was restless and could not be quiet. He prayed for peace, but sin does not give in. It hurts and causes pain. Being troubled, means that he was worried about his condition. When David <u>acknowledged</u>, <u>confessed</u> and <u>asked forgiveness,</u> he was then able to receive relief from his pain, **[Psalm 32:5, 51:3]**.

There is Forgiveness after Confession

Sin **separates** us from God **[Psalm 51:11-12]**. We see that when Adam and Eve sinned, God evicted them out of the Garden. In fact, when they sinned they hid themselves from Him. However, **Psalm 51** shows us a man who acknowledged his sin and went immediately to God for healing and forgiveness.

He said, **Create in me a clean heart, O God; and renew a right spirit within me**, **[Psalm 51:10]**. We must confess and seek God's forgiveness. God is willing and able to forgive, but we must acknowledge our sins and seek forgiveness [**I John 1:8-10**].

God **forgives** [**Isaiah 55:6-11**], and **forgets** [**Psalm 103:12**]. He is not like us who hold grudges, and governments who hold records against offenders. When we ask His forgiveness, He forgives and frees us of the burden, and guilt of sin [**I John 2:1-2**].

Suggestions for further reading

Genesis 3

Psalm 32, 38, 51

Psalm 103

Isaiah 55:6-11

I John 1:8-10

I John 2:1-2

Discussion

i.   Why do you think Adam and Eve felt naked after they had sinned?

ii. What does the deceitfulness of sin means referring to Psalm 38?

iii. Why did David say he was born in sin?

iv. How does sin destroy socially, morally, physically, and spiritually?

v.   What is the remedy for sin?

The Deceitfulness of Sin
Lesson 3: Sin Grieves the Holy Spirit

I Corinthians 6:15-20, Ephesians 4:31-32, Colossians 3:12-17

Introduction

When the believer commits sin, it grieves the Holy Spirit. The Bible teaches, **Know ye not that your body is the temple of the Holy Ghost (*which is*) in you, which ye have of God, and ye are not your own? [I Corinthians 6:19].**

We can use our bodies in many ways to sin: whether by lying against another, speaking evil, or committing sexual sins. <u>Anything</u> that is sinful will grieve the Holy Spirit, and will cause Him to leave.

The Bible instructs us, **And grieve not the Holy Spirit of God, whereby ye are sealed unto the day of redemption, [Ephesians 4:30; 1:13].**

If we sin, there is no reason to remain in that condition because God provided the requirement and process for forgiveness and cleansing.

Similar to David, each person must acknowledge sinful acts and disobedience, by confessing and turning away from the behaviour.

The Bible encourages us not to sin stating, **My little children, these things write I unto you, that ye sin not. And if any man sin, we have an advocate with the Father, Jesus Christ the righteous: And he is the propitiation for our sins: and not for ours only, but also for (*the sins of*) the whole world, [I John 2:1-2].**

Jesus came to the world to restore the relationship between God and man. It took His shed blood on Calvary to reconcile us. Since regenerated man still has the sinful nature in him, he needs someone to appease God's judgment, and Jesus is the only One who can fill this position. He is the propitiation for our sins.

Sins which *Grieve* the Holy Spirit

Bitterness: This includes resentment, anger, animosities, hostilities, spite, rancour and coldness towards another who caused hurt.

Wrath: This means violence, outbursts of anger, rage, and passion, both explicit and covert.

Anger: This can be covert or overt causing fear to others. Anger can lead to a desire for revenge, to cause punishment.

Clamour: This is noise and uproar, commotion, shouting, outcry for vengeance and so much more.

Evil Speaking: This is blasphemy or abuse against someone. This kind of behaviour hurts reputations and causes distress. People do not recognize the danger of evil speaking against another person, especially when mixed with lies. It also includes resisting the convincing power of the Holy Spirit.

Malice: This is evidence of wickedness. It is an evil act of the mind that may even cause hurt to another person, or the one for whom the malice is intended. Further, malice is hatred, malevolence, meanness and cruelty. [**See also Colossians 3:5-11**].

Behaviours which *Please* the Holy Spirit
[Ephesians 4:32, Colossians 3:12-17]

i. **Kindness** toward one another;
ii. **Forgiving** one another; patience toward one another;
iii. **Love** as you would want to be loved;
iv. **Seek peace**: blessed are the peace makers;
v. **Thankfulness**: If we show thankfulness to God, we will show the same toward one another.

_____

_____

_____

_____

_____

_____

_____

_____

_____

_____

The Deceitfulness of Sin
Lesson 4: A Call to Repentance

Isaiah 1:16-20, and 55:6-11, Joel 2

Prayer, Humility, Obedience, Repentance, Forgiveness

Despite our weaknesses and tendencies to sin and commit spiritual adultery, God is calling us to obedience and repentance. In **Isaiah 1:18** we read, **Come now, and let us reason together, saith the Lord: though your sins be as scarlet, they shall be as white as snow; though they be red like crimson, they shall be as wool.**

God loves His people, and it is not His will that any be destroyed with the world. He said, **If my people which are called by my name, shall humble themselves and pray, and seek my face, and turn from their wicked ways; then will I hear from heaven, and will forgive their sin, and will heal their land,** [II Chronicles 7:14].

God Cares

God cares for His people and He will always call them back to Him. From the moment Adam and Eve disobeyed God, He knew. Despite their weakness, He did not leave them to themselves or to the evil devices of the enemy.

Instead, God sought them out, while they hid from Him. God did not change His relationship. He did not depart from them, but continued the relationship by searching for them at the usual place in the Garden, but they were not there.

And the Lord God called unto Adam, and said unto him, Where (*art*) thou? [9]

And he said, I heard thy voice in the garden, and I was afraid, because I (*was*) naked; and I hid myself. [10]

And he said, Who told thee that you (*was*) naked? Hast thou eaten of the tree, whereof I commanded thee that thou should not eat? [11]

And the man said, The woman whom you gave (*to be*) with me, she gave me of the tree, and I did eat, [Genesis 3:9-12].

When the Holy Spirit convicts us of sin, we should not delay in making right by repenting and turning away from that offence. Sin is an offence against God, and grieves the Holy Spirit by which we are sealed.

Repentance means a change of heart or turning away from what used to be to something new. It is a change of course and intention. The responsibility is for the sinner to acknowledge his fault and seek forgiveness.

The Bible teaches we should not serve sin nor give our bodies as instruments of unrighteousness [Romans 6:13].

He that commits sin is of the devil; for the devil sinned from the beginning. For this purpose the Son of God was manifested , that he might destroy the works of the devil [I John 3:8].

God calls for Repentance: Joel 2:12-13

Therefore also now, saith the Lord, Turn ye (*even*) to me with all your heart, and with fasting, and with weeping, and with mourning. [12]

And rend your heart, and not your garments, and turn unto the Lord your God: for he is gracious and merciful, slow to anger, and of great kindness, and repents him of the evil. [13]

_____

_____

_____

_____

_____

_____

_____

_____

_____

_____

_____

_____

_____